Thames Path

National Trail Companion

supported by

5th edition published February 2007

© National Trails Office

ISBN 0-9535207-8-1

edited by Natalie Kosucu & Jos Joslin

Photographs on front cover and pages 16, 18, 32, 35, 45, 85, 89, 91, 97
© Natural England/Anne-Katrin Purkiss;

Photographs on pages 33, 43, 46, 56
© Natural England/Rob Fraser;

Photographs on pages 9, 24, 33, 40, 48, 52, 53, 79
© Jos Joslin;

Photograph on page 42
© Natural England/Archie Miles;

Photograph on page 86
© River Thames Alliance/Chris Parry

Published by
National Trails Office
Environment & Economy
Holton
Oxford OX33 1QQ

tel 01865 810224
fax 01865 810207

email Nationaltrails@oxfordshire.gov.uk
website www.nationaltrail.co.uk

Produced by Cliffehanger Ltd
tel 0113 252 6083

Designed by Linda Francis
tel 01865 407626

Cover photo by Anne-Katrin Purkiss:
Radcot

Contents

Introduction

The Thames Path follows England's best known river for 184 miles (294 km) as it meanders from its source in Gloucestershire through several rural counties and on into the bustle of the City of London. On its way the Path passes peaceful water meadows rich in wildlife, historic towns and many lovely villages, finishing at the Thames Barrier in Woolwich. Easy to reach by public transport, this National Trail can be enjoyed in many ways, whether for an afternoon's stroll, a weekend's break or a full scale, but relatively gentle, trek of its whole length.

Welcome to the Thames Path Companion. It provides up-to-date practical information about accommodation, refreshments and many other facilities along the 294 km (184 miles) of National Trail from the source of the river in Gloucestershire, through Wiltshire, Oxfordshire, Berkshire, Buckinghamshire, Surrey and into London. The Companion is designed to help with planning anything from a three week's walking holiday to an afternoon out with the dog.

The Companion is not a route guide: for detailed information of the Trail itself, **The Thames Path National Trail Guide** by David Sharp is available from most book shops. Alternatively it can be mail ordered from the National Trails Office (see page 15 for details). The Companion complements the Trail Guide and, armed with a copy of each, it is hoped that anyone using the Trail needn't require anything more. Enjoy your trip.

Opened in 1996 as one of thirteen National Trails in England, the Thames Path follows the country's best known river as it meanders from its source in the Cotswolds through several rural counties and on into the heart of London. This Trail provides level, easy walking and can be enjoyed in many ways, whether for an afternoon's stroll, a weekend's break or a full scale, but relatively gentle trek of its whole length. Another advantage is that the Thames Path can be easily reached by public transport, including an excellent network of train services the whole distance between Oxford and London.

At the start of the Path, the source of the River Thames beneath an elderly ash tree in a field in the Cotswolds, you may well find no water at all. However, gradually as you travel the trickle becomes a stream and soon a river bordered by willows and alders. As far as Oxford, apart from a couple of small historic towns and a few pleasant villages, there is a real sense of remoteness and rural tranquillity as the Thames winds its way through flat water meadows grazed by cattle or sheep, or fields of crops.

i INTRODUCTION

Beyond Oxford, the city of dreaming spires, you will still be in the heart of the countryside with its wealth of wildlife. The river whose banks you're following continues to widen, the willows seem to grow larger, and settlements become more frequent. From Goring where the Path coincides for a short distance with another National Trail, the ancient Ridgeway, the Chiltern Hills provide a wooded backdrop to your journey with their colours changing dramatically with the seasons.

When you reach Henley the Path starts to get busier with more people enjoying strolls with a dog, picnics on the bank or boating trips on the water. However, once you're away from towns or villages around a bend or two of the river, you'll regain the rural peacefulness. As the Thames Path passes beneath Windsor Castle, you are reminded that you are following a Royal river; the palaces of Hampton Court and Kew a little further downstream confirm this.

From the last non-tidal lock on the Thames at Teddington, you can choose to walk on either the north or the south bank of the river through most of London. You'll pass leafy Richmond and Kew, remarkably green areas, before entering the heart of the City with its many famous buildings bordering the Thames. The final few miles to the finish at the Thames Barrier take you amongst restored warehouses and the working wharves in London's Docklands.

With the support of Natural England, the Thames Path is managed to the highest standards necessary for one of the most important paths in the country by the local highway authorities with a small dedicated team of National Trails staff and volunteers.

The Thames Valley was originally settled by prehistoric people with the earliest occupations discovered so far dating from the New Stone Age, some 6 000 years ago. These are at Runnymede and Staines near the Thames, not far from present day London. The river has been a very important trading route for hundreds of years and it was only during the latter half of the twentieth century that it mostly ceased to carry goods. Nowadays leisure boats rather than barges are the main users of the Thames.

It was in medieval times that the river became increasingly important for trade, especially in those days for carrying wool from the lush Cotswold meadows to London. St Paul's Cathedral is built of Taynton stone quarried in the Cotswolds and carried to London by barges towed by men and horses from Radcot. By the 18th century London was the world's busiest port and Reading, for example, received 95% of its goods by barge towed along the River Thames.

The towpath between Lechlade and Putney, along which much of the Thames Path now travels, was established towards the end of the 18th century by the Thames Commissioners at a time when the country's new canal system was being built which connected the Thames to other parts of Britain. It was a difficult task since many landowners refused permission for the towing path to enter their land or there were natural obstacles in its way. As a result in many places the towpath switched from one bank of the river to the other and ferries were used to transfer the towing horses across the river. When the commercial traffic died as a result of competition from the railways so did the navigation ferries.

This created a major problem for the setting up of the Thames Path. Either bridges had to be built where the old ferries used to operate or alternative routes to the towpath had to be found.

iii WILDLIFE

Wherever you walk along the Thames Path there should be plenty of wildlife to observe and enjoy although, of course, the time of year you are there is important. There will be birds present all year round, but if you're keen on wild flowers then April to September is the time to visit, and if insects are an interest of yours choose June to September.

Plants of the riverside seem to be especially colourful from the bright yellow of the flag iris and marsh marigold in spring to the pinks of the willowherbs and purple loosestrife during summer. Plants of particular note along the Path are the nationally rare Loddon lily and snakeshead fritillary, both flowering on a few flood meadows in early spring.

Insects are in abundance during the summer when dragonflies and damselflies, amongst the largest and so most noticeable, are active. There are various species, many wonderfully coloured and you'll be able to watch them mating, laying eggs, hunting for food or patrolling their territories.

Snakeshead fritillaries

Of the mammals you'll no doubt see rabbits and maybe a stoat or a weasel. Unfortunately you're unlikely to see an otter, a relative of the latter, although thankfully they are returning to the upper reaches of the Thames and perhaps in the future will be more plentiful and obvious. Another animal in trouble is the water vole, 'Ratty' of Kenneth Grahame's 'Wind in the Willows'. They used to be very common on the Thames emerging from their holes in the bank and busily ploughing backwards and forwards across the river, but their numbers have crashed in recent years. Let us know if and where you spot one.

The most obvious animals are the birds, many of which being water birds are large and thankfully don't fly away as soon as you appear! The majestic mute swan has to be the symbol of the Thames and is increasingly common thanks to the ban in the 1980s on anglers using lead weights. Swans eating these weights in mistake for the grit they need to take in to break down plant material in their gizzards were poisoned and killed and their numbers diminished considerably.

Wherever you go you'll see the commonest of Britain's ducks, the mallard, which like all ducks is especially resplendent from October to March. But other species of ducks visit the river too, so look out for tufted duck, pochard and wigeon. Geese, larger relatives of ducks, also abound in places, usually found in large noisy flocks grazing in fields near the river or roosting on the water itself. The Canada goose is very common.

The Thames Path is primarily a route for use by walkers, although in a few places, especially in towns and cities and near London, cyclists can use sections. In a few places horseriders, too, can share the Path.

Spring, summer and autumn months are the best time to enjoy the Thames Path since there is very little risk of the river flooding and making the Trail impassable.

Be prepared!

Whenever venturing into the countryside it is wise to be prepared for the elements: even in summer, wind and rain can make a walk cold and uncomfortable, so suitable warm and waterproof clothing should be worn or carried in a small rucksack. After rain, and particularly during winter, the Trail can be muddy, so wear strong, comfortable and waterproof footwear.

During winter months and occasionally at other times, some sections of the Path, especially in the upper reaches, can become flooded and unwalkable after heavy rain. To be sure of keeping your feet dry telephone the **Environment Agency's flood information line on 08459 881188.**

 ## Dog Matters

If you are planning to undertake a long distance walk along the Thames Path with your dog, you are advised to ensure it is fit before you start; on occasions walkers have had to abandon a walk because their dogs can't keep up!

Please also make sure your dog is under close control at all times to prevent it from disturbing livestock or wildlife. Whilst in fields with livestock you are asked to keep your dog on a lead, although on occasions cattle may harass you because of the dog and in such circumstances it may be wise to let it off the lead.

Signing

The Thames Path follows a series of well-signed public rights of way along which people have a legal right of access.

An acorn, the symbol of Britain's National Trails, is used to guide your journey by marking the route in a variety of ways. It is used in conjunction with coloured arrows or the words 'footpath', 'bridleway' or 'byway' to indicate who can use a particular right of way.

The word 'footpath' and/or a yellow arrow indicates a path for use by walkers only and where, without the landowner's permission, it is illegal to cycle, ride a horse or drive a vehicle. Outside London, 83% of the Thames Path is footpath.

The word 'bridleway' and/or a blue arrow indicates a path which can be used by walkers, horseriders and cyclists but where, without the landowner's permission, it is illegal to drive any vehicle. Outside London, 6% of the Thames Path is bridleway.

The word 'byway' and/or a red arrow indicates a right of way which can be legally used by walkers, horseriders, cyclists and motorists. Outside London, 0.7% of the Thames Path is byway.

The Thames Path is signposted where it crosses roads and many rights of way using wooden or metal signposts. Elsewhere, waymark discs with acorns and coloured arrows are used on gates, stiles and waymark posts.

Guides

The Thames Path National Trail Guide by David Sharp, Aurum Press – the official Guide with written route description and colour maps.

Maps

It is always a good idea to use an Ordnance Survey map when walking, particularly in unfamiliar areas. The National Trail Guide includes colour sections of all the appropriate 1:25 000 maps needed to follow the Thames Path. Alternatively, for you to enjoy and interpret the wider landscape, you may wish to purchase your own maps.

The Landranger series (pink cover at 1:50 000 or 2 cm to 1 km) has all public rights of way, viewpoints, tourist information and selected places of interest marked on them.

The larger scale Explorer series (orange cover at 1:25 000 or 4 cm to 1 km) has more detail including fence lines which can be very helpful when following rights of way, recreational routes and greater tourist information.

Landranger		Explorer	
163	Cheltenham & Cirencester	168	Stroud, Tetbury & Malmesbury
164	Oxford	169	Cirencester and Swindon
174	Newbury and Wantage	170	Abingdon, Wantage and Vale of
175	Reading and Windsor		White Horse
176	West London	180	Oxford
177	East London	171	Chiltern Hills West
		172	Chiltern Hills East
		160	Windsor, Weybridge and Bracknell
		161	London South
		173	London North
		162	Greenwich and Gravesend

Publications about the Thames Path and River

There are many publications available about the River Thames and its Path of which the following is a selection:

The Thames Path National Trail Guide by David Sharp, Aurum Press 2005 (new edition due 2007) – the official guide with written route description and colour maps.

Thames: the River and the Path GEOprojects, 2006 – a fold-out map at a scale of 1:60 000.

Walks Along the Thames Path by Ron Emmons, 2006 – 25 circular walks from Thames Head to Greenwich.

The Thames Path by Leigh Hatts, Cicerone Press 2005

Pubs of the River Thames by Mark Turner, Prion Books 2004 – colour pictures and details of over 100 pubs beside the Thames from the Cotswolds to London's East End.

Rambling for Pleasure along the Thames East Berkshire Ramblers Group 1999 – short circular walks (all less than 6 miles) between Runnymede and Sonning.

Pub Walks along the Thames Path by Leigh Hatts, Countryside Books 1997 – 20 circular walks.

The Secret Thames by Duncan Mackay, Ebury Press/Countryside Commission 1996

Chilterns and Thames Valley Walks Ordnance Survey Pathfinder Guide 1994

The Thames Path by Helen Livingstone, Aerofilms Guide 1993 – aerial photographs illustrating the route of the path.

Walks along the Thames Path by Leigh Hatts, Patrick Stephens Ltd 1990 – circular walks incorporating the Thames Path.

A Walk along the River Thames by Gareth Huw Davies, Michael Joseph 1990

Sea to Source – London Weekend Television 2002 – VHS video T: 020 7827 7563

World's Most Beautiful Waterways – The Thames Contender Entertainment 2000 – VHS video, introduced by David Suchet

Walking the Thames Path from Sea to Source by Leigh Hatts, 2005 – A guide for those walking the Thames Path upstream.

The following companies offer self-guided or guided holiday packages on part or all of the Thames Path:

Walking

Contours Walking Holidays, Gramyre, 3 Berrier Close, Greystoke, CA11 0UB **T**: 01768 480451, www.contours.co.uk

Xplore Britain, 6 George Street, Ferryhill, DL17 0DT **T**: 01740 650900, www.xplorebritain.com

Freedom Walking Holidays, 4 Almond Court, Swanpool, Lincoln LN6 0HD **T**: 01522 684104, www.freedom-walking.co.uk

HF Holidays, HF Holidays, Imperial House, The Hyde, Edgware Road, London, NW9 5AL **T**: 0208 905 9558, www.hfholidays.co.uk

Instep Walking Holidays, 35 Cokeham Road, Lancing, West Sussex, BN15 0AE **T**: 01903 766475, www.instephols.co.uk

Boating/Walking

Kari UK, Wharf 315, Thames Path Walking Holidays, 266 Banbury Road, Summertown, Oxford, OX2 7DL T: 07970 939725, www.kariuk.com

Please note for those visiting the Thames Path independently many of the accommodation providers listed in this guide are willing to collect you from and return you to the Trail. Many will also transport your luggage to your next night's accommodation.

Thames Path Managers

National Trails Officers, Margaret Caddick and Jos Joslin, Environment & Economy, Holton, Oxford OX33 1QQ **T**: 01865 810224 **F**: 01865 810207 **E**: Nationaltrails@oxfordshire.gov.uk

Highway Authorities responsible for public rights of way

Buckinghamshire County Council, Planning and Environment, County Hall, Walton Street, AYLESBURY HP20 1UY **T**: 01296 395000 www.buckscc.gov.uk

Gloucestershire County Council, Environment Dept, Shire Hall, Westgate Street, GLOUCESTER GL1 2TH **T**: 01452 425577 www.gloucestershire.gov.uk **E**: prow@gloucestershire.gov.uk

Oxfordshire County Council, Countryside Service, Environment & Economy, Holton, OXFORD OX33 1QQ **T**: 01865 810226 www.oxfordshire.gov.uk

Reading Borough Council, Rights of Way Dept, Civic Offices, READING RG1 7TD **T**: 01189 390900 www.reading.gov.uk

Royal Borough of Windsor and Maidenhead, Development and Transport Section, Town Hall, St Ives Road, Maidenhead SL6 1RF **T**: 01628 798888 www.rbwm.gov.uk

Surrey County Council, Sustainable Development, County Hall, KINGSTON KT1 2DY **T**: 08456 009 009 www.surreycc.gov.uk

Swindon Borough Council, Environment and Leisure, 2nd Floor, Premier House, Station Road, SWINDON SN1 1TZ **T**: 01793 463000 www.swindon.gov.uk

West Berkshire Council, Countryside and Environment, Faraday Road, NEWBURY RG14 2AF **T**: 01635 42400 www.westberks.gov.uk

Wiltshire County Council, Dept of Environmental Services, County Hall, TROWBRIDGE, BA14 8JD **T**: 01225 713000 www.wiltshire.gov.uk

Wokingham District Council, Environment Services, Civic Offices, Shute End, WOKINGHAM RG40 1BN **T**: 0118 974 6000 www.wokingham.gov.uk

Agency responsible for National Trails

Natural England, National Trails, 20th Floor, Portland House LONDON SW1E 5RS
T: 020 7932 5899   www.naturalengland.org.uk

Agency responsible for the River Thames

Environment Agency, Isis House, WALLINGFORD OX10 8BD **T**: 08708 506 506
www.environment-agency.gov.uk **E**: enquiries@environment-agency.gov.uk

Environment Agency's Flood Information **T**: 08459 881188

Weathercall (up-to-date weather forecasts)

	Telephone Numbers
Sections 1&2 (Wiltshire and Gloucestershire)	09068 505305
Sections 3–11 (Oxfordshire, Berkshire and Buckinghamshire)	09068 505306
Sections 11&12 (Surrey)	09068 505302
Sections 13–15 (London)	09068 505301

OR www.met-office.gov.uk (The areas covering the Thames Path are:
South-East England & the West Country)

Chiltern Hills from Gatehampton

The Thames Path is exceptionally well served by public transport which makes it possible to explore the Trail without needing a car by using trains, buses or, unusually for a National Trail, boats.

A free leaflet summarising the bus, train and boat services to the Trail is available from the National Trails Office (see page 15 for details).

Rail Services
For information:
National Rail Enquiries **T**: 08457 484950 (24 hours a day)
www.nationalrail.co.uk or www.networkrail.co.uk

Bus Services
For information:
National Public Transport Information Service **T**: 0870 608 2608
Traveline www.traveline.org.uk

Public Transport in London
For information:
London Travel Information **T**: 020 7222 1234 www.tfl.gov.uk

Details of taxi services are included at the beginning of each section.

x RESPECT THE COUNTRYSIDE

• **Be safe – plan ahead and follow any signs**

Even when going out locally, it's best to get the latest information about where and when you can go. Follow advice and local signs, and be prepared for the unexpected.

• **Leave gates and property as you find them**

Please respect the working life of the countryside, as our actions can affect people's livelihoods, our heritage, and the safety and welfare of animals and ourselves.

• **Protect plants and animals, and take your litter home**

We have a responsibility to protect our countryside now and for future generations, so make sure you don't harm animals, birds, plants or trees.

• **Keep your dog under close control**

The countryside is a great place to exercise dogs, but it's every owner's duty to make sure their dog is not a danger or nuisance to farm animals, wildlife or other people.

• **Consider other people**

Showing consideration and respect for other people makes the countryside a pleasant environment for everyone – at home, at work and at leisure.

For further details visit www.countrysideaccess.gov.uk

Goring-on-Thames

In emergency dial 999 and ask for the service required.

Police

These numbers are for non-emergencies. Telephone the number for the county you are in and ask to be put through to the nearest police station.

Section	County	Telephone Numbers
1&3	Gloucestershire	0845 090 1234
1&2	Wiltshire	0845 408 7000
3–11	Berkshire, Oxfordshire & Buckinghamshire	08458 505 505
11&12	Surrey	0845 125 2222
13–15	Greater London	0207 230 1212
14	City of London	0207 601 2222

Hospitals

The telephone numbers given are for the hospital switchboard; ask to be put through to Accident & Emergency Reception.

◆   Full 24-hour emergency service

▼   Minor injuries only, 24-hour service

Section	Town/City	Telephone No	Address
1	◆ Cirencester	01285 655711	Cirencester Hospital, the Querns, Tetbury Road, Cirencester
1,2 & 3	◆ Swindon	01793 604020	The Great Western Hospital, Marlborough Road, Swindon
3,4 & 5	◆ Oxford	01865 741166	John Radcliffe Hospital, Headley Way, Headington, Oxford

Hospitals cont.

Section	Town/City	Telephone No	Address
6 & 7	▼ Wallingford	01491 208500	Wallingford Community Hospital, Reading Road, Wallingford
7 & 8	◆ Reading	0118 987 5111	The Royal Berkshire Hospital, London Road, Reading
8 & 9	▼ Henley	01491 637400	Townlands Hospital, York Rd, Henley-on-Thames
9 & 10	◆ High Wycombe	01494 526161	Wycombe General Hospital, Queen Alexandra Road, High Wycombe
10 & 11	◆ Slough	01753 633000	Wexham Park Hospital, Wexham Street, Slough
11 & 12	◆ Chertsey	01932 872000	St Peter's Hospital, Guildford Road, Chertsey
12	◆ Kingston-upon-Thames	020 8546 7711	Kingston Hospital, Galsworthy Road, Kingston-upon-Thames
13	◆ Isleworth	020 8560 2121	West Middlesex University Hospital, Twickenham Road, Isleworth
13 & 14	◆ Hammersmith	020 8846 1234	Charing Cross Hospital, Fulham Palace Road, London W6
14	◆ Chelsea	020 8746 8000	Chelsea & Westminster Hospital, 369 Fulham Road, London SW10
14	◆ Lambeth	020 7188 7188	St Thomas's Hospital, Lambeth Palace Road, London SE1
14 & 15	▼ The City	020 7188 7188	Guy's Hospital, St Thomas Street, London SE1
15	◆ Dartford	01322 428100	Darent Valley Hospital, Darent Wood Road, Dartford

Accommodation, Facilities & Services

This booklet gives details of the settlements, accommodation, eating places, shops, attractions and other facilities along the Thames Path. They are listed in geographic order from the source of the river to the Thames Barrier in London.

If you fail to find accommodation using this guide please contact the Tourist Information Centres listed near the beginning of each section which may be able to provide other addresses. Some towns and cities, including London, have such an extensive range and number of places to stay that details of individual establishments are not listed in this guide.

The Thames Path is divided into fifteen sections as indicated on the map on page 4. At the start of each section is a map showing the settlements close to the Trail within that section. These maps are meant only as a guide and you are recommended to use this Companion in conjunction with the Thames Path National Trail Guide or maps.

You are strongly advised to book accommodation in advance. Whilst booking, do check prices since those quoted here are usually the minimum charged.

For those who would like to enjoy more than a day on the Thames Path without having to carry all their possessions, quite a few accommodation providers have indicated whether they are willing to transport the luggage you don't need during the day to your next night's accommodation. The fee charged for this service needs to be discussed and agreed at the time of the booking. Accommodation providers have also indicated if they are willing to collect you from the Thames Path and deliver you back after your stay.

All the information within this Companion is as accurate as possible. Inclusion of accommodation does not constitute a recommendation although it is indicated in the details whether an establishment has a recognised grade awarded to it. If you have any comments or notice any errors, please write to Jos Joslin the National Trails Manager responsible for this guide (page 15).

Key to Symbols for Settlements

Any comments relate to preceding icon.

- map grid reference (see start of each section for relevant maps)
- shortest walking distance from the Thames Path
- most convenient train station
- **P£** car park (paying)
- **PF** car park (free)
- telephone
- toilets
- **WC** toilets adapted for disabled users
- Tourist Information Centre
- pub (usually open lunchtimes 11am-3pm then evenings 6pm-11pm). Names and telephone numbers of pubs are given for those settlements with two or fewer pubs
- bar meals in pub
- post office (usual opening hours 9am-5.30pm weekdays; 9am-12.30pm Sat)
- general store (usual opening hours 9am-5.30pm Mon-Sat)
- cafe/tea shop
- restaurant
- food take-away

S M T W T F S opening hours of services relate to the preceding symbol

eg: ▯ open all day   ▮ closed all day

▯ Post offices, general stores, cafe/tea shops – open morning; Pubs, bar meals, restaurants, takeaways – open lunchtime

▮ Post offices, general stores, cafe/tea shops – open afternoon; Pubs, bar meals, restaurants, takeaways – open evening

- **£** bank (usually open daily 9.30am-4.30pm Mon-Fri)
- cash machine available, including outside bank opening hours
- ☆ tourist attraction

Key to Symbols for Accommodation

Type of accommodation (symbols in margins)

yha	youth hostel	H	hotel
Λ	camping	INN	inn
SC	self catering		

The number and price following the symbols for rooms gives the number and price of that type of room available. The same applies to tent/caravan pitches. Prices quoted for rooms are the minimum price per room per night for bed and breakfast. The price for single occupancy of double, twin or family rooms is given in brackets eg (£22.00).

Accommodation symbols – hotels, inns, guest houses, B&Bs and youth hostels

- double room
- twin room
- family room
- single room
- no smoking in bedrooms
- children welcome
- wheelchair access
- dogs allowed by arrangement
- V caters for vegetarians
- packed lunches available

- evening meals available at accommodation or locally
- DRY clothes/boots drying facilities
- laundry facilities
- transport to and from Trail by arrangement
- luggage transported to next overnight stop by arrangement
- VISA credit card(s) accepted
- ◆ VisitBritain accommodation standard for B&Bs, guest houses, inns
- ★ VisitBritain accommodation standard for hotels
- special feature/comment

Accommodation symbols – camping and caravan sites

🏕	tent pitches		🚿	showers
🚐	caravan pitches		📞	public telephone
🚰	cold water		⬜	laundry facilities
🚰	hot water		🏪	site shop
🚻	toilets		CG	camping gas available
♿WC	toilets adapted for disabled users			special feature/comment

Close to the source of the Thames

Section

1

The Source to Cricklade

This rural first 12 miles (20km) of the Thames Path is within the fine countryside of the Cotswolds where farming and small stone-built settlements dominate. The river grows from nothing to a narrow waterway by the time it reaches Cricklade.

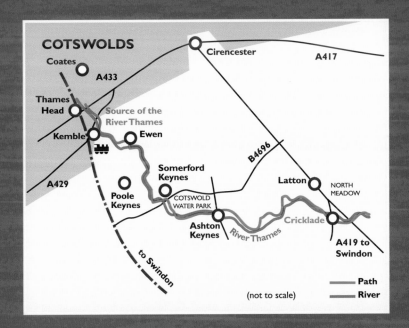

COTSWOLDS

Coates

A433

Cirencester

A417

Thames Head

Source of the River Thames

Kemble

Ewen

B4696

Somerford Keynes

Latton

NORTH MEADOW

A429

Poole Keynes

COTSWOLD WATER PARK

Ashton Keynes

River Thames

Cricklade

A419 to Swindon

to Swindon

(not to scale)

Path
River

Maps

Landranger maps	163	Cheltenham & Cirencester
Explorer maps	168	Stroud, Tetbury & Malmesbury
	169	Cirencester & Swindon

Taxi Services

Place	Name	Telephone numbers
Cirencester	A2B Taxis	01285 655651
	Cirencester Taxis	01285 642767
	Monarch Taxis	01285 656871
	AAR Services	01285 658189
Cricklade	Abbey Taxis	01666 826072
	A.S.T Ltd	01666 823388

Car Parking

The following is a list of public car parks close to the Thames Path and does not include on-street parking in villages or towns. Where there are several car parks in a town, those closest to the Path have been listed. Unfortunately theft from vehicles parked in the countryside does occasionally occur, so please leave valuables you don't want to carry at home.

Place	Map Grid Reference
Neigh Bridge Country Park, off Spine Road West 1/2 mile south of Somerford Keynes	SU 018947
Waterhay Bridge, 1 mile southeast of Ashton Keynes	SU 060933
Cricklade Town Hall	SU 100935

Toilets

Place	Map Grid Reference
Neigh Bridge Country Park – summers only	SU 018947
Cricklade, off High Street ♿	SU 100937

Tourist Information Centres

*Offers accommodation booking service for personal callers during opening hours

Place	Address/Opening Hours
*Cirencester	Corn Hall, Market Place, Cirencester GL7 2NW T: 01285 654180 F: 01285 641182 www.cotswold.gov.uk **Opening hours** Summer (Apr-end Dec): Mon 9:45-17:30, Tue-Sat 9:30-17:30 Winter (Jan-end Mar): Mon 9:45-17:00, Tue-Sat 9:30-17:00
*Swindon	37 Regent Street, Swindon SN1 1JL T: 01793 530328 F: 01793 434031 **Opening hours** All year: Mon-Sat 9:15-17:00

CIRENCESTER

 SP0201 3miles (5km)
Kemble 5miles (8km)

Town with full range of services; visit www.cirencester.gov.uk for further details. Cirencester has a wide range of accommodation – details from Tourist Information Centre (see section introduction).

☆ Corinium Museum
T: 01285 655611

☆ Brewery Arts Centre
T: 01285 657181

☆ Roman Amphitheatre
T: 01179 750700

COATES

SP9801 1.3miles (2km)
Kemble 3.4miles (5.5km)

S M T W T F S S M T W T F S

Pub: The Tunnel House Inn 01285 770280

THAMES HEAD

SU9898 on path
Kemble 1.2miles (2km)

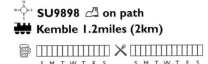
S M T W T F S S M T W T F S

Pub: Thames Head Inn 01285 770259

KEMBLE

 **ST9897** 🛏 **0.5miles (1km)**
🚂 **Kemble P£** 📞

🍺 ▯▯▯▯▯▯▯▯▯▯▯ ✕ ▯▯▯▯▯▯▯▯▯▯▯▯
S M T W T F S   S M T W T F S

✉ ▮▯▯▯▯▯▯ 🧺 ▯▯▯▯▯▯▯▯▯▯▯▯
S M T W T F S   S M T W T F S

£ Inside village shop
Pub: Tavern 01285 770216

EWEN

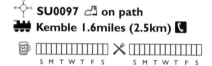 **SU0097** 🛏 **on path**
🚂 **Kemble 1.6miles (2.5km)** 📞

🍺 ▯▯▯▯▯▯▯▯▯▯▯ ✕ ▯▯▯▯▯▯▯▯▯▯▯▯
S M T W T F S   S M T W T F S

Pub: Wild Duck Inn 01285 770310
☆ Cirencester Park
T: 01285 653135

Brooklands Farm

Mrs E M Crew
Ewen, Cirencester GL7 6BU
T: 01285 770487
🛏 1 £50 🛏 1 £50 (£25) 🚭 **V** **DRY**
🚗 👣 ◆◆◆

The Wild Duck   *Closed Xmas night*

Mrs Tina Mussell
Ewen, Cirencester GL7 6BY
T: 01285 770310 **F:** 01285 770924
E: wduckinn@aol.com
www.thewildduckinn.co.uk
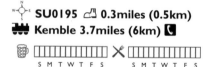 🛏 6 £95 (£70) 🛏 6 £70 🌙 👫 ♿
📷 **V** 🖊 🚭 🚗 👣 VISA Mastercard,
Visa, American Express ★★ All rooms
en-suite
▌ Twelve rooms in total; can be either
single or double

SOMERFORD KEYNES

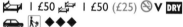 **SU0195** 🛏 **0.3miles (0.5km)**
🚂 **Kemble 3.7miles (6km)** 📞

🍺 ▯▯▯▯▯▯▯▯▯▯▯ ✕ ▯▯▯▯▯▯▯▯▯▯▯▯
S M T W T F S   S M T W T F S

Pub: Baker's Arms 01285 861298.
Self-catering holiday accommodation
available: 1) Thames Path Cottages **T:**
01285 644416 **E:** info@thames-path-
cottages.co.uk 2) Lower Mill Holiday
Homes **T:** 01285 861839
E: bookings@orionholidays.com

☆ Cotswold Water Park
T: 01285 861459 **E:** info@waterpark.org
www.waterpark.org

POOLE KEYNES

⊕ **SU0095** 🥾 **0.8miles (1.3km)**
🚂 **Kemble 2.4miles (3.8km)** 📞

Self-catering holiday accommodation
available: Old Mill Cottages
T: 01285 821255
E: catherine@oldmillcottages.fsnet.co.uk

Cotswold Willow Pool

Mrs Vivienne Jones
Oaksey Road, Poole Keynes,
Cirencester GL7 6DZ
T: 01285 861485 **M:** 07980 501049
E: jones.willow@btopenworld.com
www.willowpool.com
🛏 2 £54 🛏 1 £58 (£40) 🚫 ♯♦V
DRY 👣 🚘♦♦♦♦ Some rooms en-suite

⊩ Visit Britain Silver Award

ASHTON KEYNES

⊕ **SU0494** 🥾 **on path**
🚂 **Kemble 5.7miles (9.2km) PF** 📞

🍺 ▯▯▯▯▯▯▯▯▯▯▯ ✕ ▯▯▯▯▯▯▯▯▯▯▯
   S M T W T F S   S M T W T F S

✉ ▮▮▮▮▯▯▯▯▯▯▯ 🍴 ▮▮▮▯▯▯▯▯▯▯▯
   S M T W T F S   S M T W T F S

Pubs: White Hart Inn 01285 861247 or
Horse and Jockey 01285 861270

☆ Cotswold Water Park
T: 01285 861459 **E:** info@waterpark.org
www.waterpark.org

Wheatleys Farm

Mrs Gill Freeth
High Road, Ashton Keynes, Swindon
SN6 6NX
T/F: 01285 861310
E: gill@wheatleysfarm.co.uk
www.wheatleysfarm.co.uk
🛏 1 £50 🛏 1 £50 (£35) 🚫 ♯♦
(min age 10) V 🖧 **DRY** 🔟 👣 ★★★★
All rooms en-suite
⊩ Family room also available - price on
application

The Firs

Ms Karen Shaw
High Road, Ashton Keynes, Swindon
SN6 6NX
T: 01285 860169 **M:** 07989 857435
E: thefirsbb@yahoo.co.uk
🛏 2 £48 🛏 1 £48 (£35) 🛏 2 £32
🚫 ♯♦ 📷 V 🖧 👣 ♦♦♦ Some rooms
en-suite

1 Cove House *Closed Xmas & New Year*

Mrs V Threlfall
Ashton Keynes, Swindon SN6 6NS
T/F: 01285 861226
E: roger@covehouse.co.uk
www.covehouse.co.uk
🛏 1 £65 🛏 1 £65 (£45) 🚫 ♯♦ V
🖧 **DRY** 🔟 👣 All rooms en-suite

LATTON

SU0995 1.6miles (2.5km)
Swindon 9.3miles (15km)

Dolls House

Mrs Gemma Maraffi
The Street, Latton, Cricklade SN6 6DJ
T/F: 01793 750384 **M:** 07762 619049
E: info@thedollshouse-bedandbreakfast.co.uk
www.thedollshouse-bedandbreakfast.co.uk
1 £55 1 £55 (£35) 1 £35
(min age 14) V DRY
Mastercard, Visa, Delta
★★★ All rooms en-suite

CRICKLADE

SU0993 on path
Swindon 7.8miles (12.5km)

Small town with full range of services;
visit www.cricklade-tc.gov.uk for further
details

☆ Cricklade Museum
T: 01793 750756

☆ North Meadow National Nature
Reserve
E: wiltshire@english-nature.org.uk
www.english-nature.org.uk

☆ Swindon & Cricklade Railway
T: 01793 771615
www.swindon-cricklade-railway.org

White Hart Hotel

Mr Britton
High Street, Cricklade SN6 6AA
T: 01793 750206 **F:** 01793 750650
E: whitehart@arkells.com
www.arkells.com
8 £65 4 £65 (£45) 2
£90 2 £45 V
Mastercard, Visa, American Express,
Delta, Maestro/Switch ◆◆◆◆ All
rooms en-suite

Cricklade Hotel & Country Club
Closed Xmas & Boxing Day

Mr Paul Butler
Common Hill, Cricklade SN6 6HA
T: 01793 750751 **F:** 01793 751767
E: reception@crickladehotel.co.uk
www.crickladehotel.co.uk
35 £115 8 £115 2 £130
5 £90 V DRY
Mastercard, Visa, American Express,
Delta. All rooms en-suite

Cottages in Cricklade

Section 2

Cricklade to Lechlade

This 11 miles (18km) of quiet countryside between the two small rural towns sees the River Thames grow to a respectable body of water with boats regularly using the final short stretch before Lechlade.

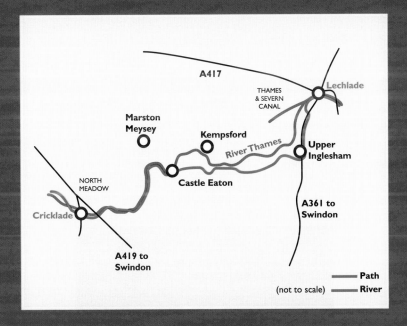

A417

THAMES & SEVERN CANAL

Lechlade

Marston Meysey

Kempsford

River Thames

Upper Inglesham

NORTH MEADOW

Castle Eaton

Cricklade

A419 to Swindon

A361 to Swindon

Path

(not to scale)   River

Maps

Landranger maps	163	Cheltenham & Cirencester
Explorer maps	169	Cirencester & Swindon
	170	Abingdon, Wantage & Vale of White Horse

Taxi Services

Place	Name	Telephone numbers
Lechlade	CTs	01367 252575
	Bampton Castle Cars	01993 851007

Car Parking

The following is a list of public car parks close to the Thames Path and does not include on-street parking in villages or towns. Where there are several car parks in a town, those closest to the Path have been listed. Unfortunately theft from vehicles parked in the countryside does occasionally occur, so please leave valuables you don't want to carry at home.

Place	Map Grid Reference
Cricklade Town Hall	SU 100935
Lechlade Riverside, on A361 ¹/2 mile south of Lechlade	SU 211990

Toilets

Place	Map Grid Reference
Cricklade, off High Street ♿	SU 100937
Lechlade Riverside park ♿	SU 211990
Lechlade, St John's Lock	SU 222990

Tourist Information Centres

*Offers accommodation booking service for personal callers during opening hours

Place	Address/Opening Hours
*Swindon	37 Regent Street, Swindon SN1 1JL **T**: 01793 530328 **F**: 01793 434031 **Opening hours:** All year: Mon-Sat 9:15-17:00
*Faringdon	The Pump House, 5 Market Place, Faringdon SN7 7HL **T/F**: 01367 242191 www.visitvale.co.uk **Opening hours:** Summer (Easter-Oct 31): Mon-Fri 09:30-16:30; Sat 09:30-13:00 Winter (Nov 1-Easter) Mon-Sat 09:30-13:00

CASTLE EATON

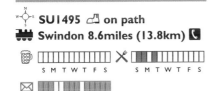

SU1495 ⌂ on path

Swindon 8.6miles (13.8km)

Pubs: Red Lion 01285 810280

The Malt House

Mrs Tayma Wallbridge
The Street, Castle Eaton SN6 6JZ
T: 01285 810822
E: tjwallbridge@supanet.com
🛏 1 £60 (£30) 🚭 V 🚿 DRY
All rooms en-suite

The Red Lion   INN

Mrs Melody-Ann Lyall
The Street, Castle Eaton SN6 6JZ
T/F: 01285 810280
E: m.lyall@btconnect.com
www.red-lion.co.uk
🛏 2 £60 🛏 1 £60 (£49) 🛏 1
£120 🚭 ♀♂ V 🚿 🍳 DRY 🚗 🐕 💳
Mastercard, Visa, Delta. Some rooms
en-suite

Hawthorn

MARSTON MEYSEY

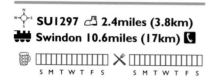

SU1297 🏞 **2.4miles (3.8km)**
🚌 **Swindon 10.6miles (17km)** 📞

🍺 |||||||||||| ✗ ||||||||||||
  S M T W T F S   S M T W T F S

Pub: The Spotted Cow 01285 810264

Second Chance Touring Park
Closed Dec-Feb

Mrs B Stroud
Second Chance, Marston Meysey SN6 6SZ
T: 01285 810675

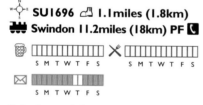

⛺ 26 £5 🚐 26 £10 🚿 🚰 👫♿WC
🏠 ★★

KEMPSFORD

SU1696 🏞 **1.1miles (1.8km)**
🚌 **Swindon 11.2miles (18km) PF** 📞

🍺 |||||||||||| ✗ ||||||||||||
  S M T W T F S   S M T W T F S

✉ |||||||||||
  S M T W T F S

Pubs: Axe and Compass 01285 810506
& George 01285 810236

Kempsford Manor

Mrs Z I Williamson
High Street, Kempsford, Fairford GL7 4EQ
T: 01285 810131 **M:** 07980 543882
E: ipek@kempsfordmanor.co.uk
www.kempsfordmanor.co.uk

🛏 2 £60 (£35) 🛏 1 £75 🛏 2 £35
🚭 ⛄ 📺 V 🔥 🌫 **DRY** 🗐 🚗 ◆◆◆
Some rooms en-suite
🍴 Evening meal by prior arrangement

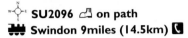

UPPER INGLESHAM

☗ **SU2096** 👢 **on path**

🚂 **Swindon 9miles (14.5km)** 📞

✕ ▮▮▮▮▮▮▮▮▮▮
S M T W T F S

Evergreen

Mr & Mrs Blowen
3 College Farm Cottages, Upper
Inglesham, Swindon SN6 7QU
T: 01367 253407
E: ingridgreen1947@hotmail.com
www.evergreen-cotswold.co.uk
🛏 1 £55 🛏 2 £33 🚭 ✝✝ (min age
14) 🔥 **DRY** 🐾

LECHLADE

☗ **SU2199** 👢 **on path**

🚂 **Swindon 10.9miles (17.5km)**

Small town with full range of services;
for further details visit www.
lechladeonthames.co.uk

☆ Lechlade Trout Farm
T: 01367 253266 www.lechladetrout.
co.uk

Cambrai Lodge

Mr John Titchener
Oak Street, Lechlade GL7 3AY
T: 01367 253173 **M:** 07860 150467
E: cambrailodge@btconnect.com
www.cambrailodgeguesthouse.co.uk
🛏 2 £50 🛏 2 £55 (£40) 🛏 1 £55
🛏 2 £30 🚭 ✝✝ 📺 V 🔥 **DRY** 🅿 🐾
◆◆◆◆ Some rooms en-suite
🛏 Additional £15 per child charge for
the family room

Bridge House Camp Site ⛺
Closed Nov-March

Mr R Cooper
Bridge House, Thames St, Lechlade GL7
3AG
T/F: 01367 252348
⛺ 30 £5 🚐 21 £5 🍴 🚿 🚰 🚻
♿WC 📱🖨
🛏 Prices are per person/night

The Round House,
upstream of Lechlade

Section 3

Lechlade to Newbridge

This 16miles (26km) is the longest section of the Thames Path following the ever-growing river as it slowly winds its way through the flat flood plain of the Thames Valley. It is wonderfully remote and therefore a good section to explore for those wanting peace and quiet, large skies and long views.

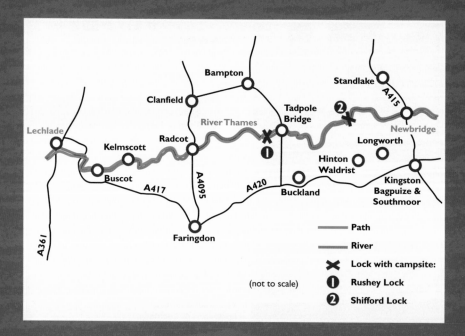

Bampton

Standlake

Clanfield

River Thames

Tadpole
Bridge

A415

②

Lechlade

Radcot

Newbridge

Kelmscott

Longworth

Buscot

A417

A4095

A420

Hinton
Waldrist

Buckland

Kingston
Bagpuize &
Southmoor

A361

Faringdon

(not to scale)

———— Path

———— River

✖ Lock with campsite:
❶ Rushey Lock
❷ Shifford Lock

Maps

Landranger maps	163	Cheltenham & Cirencester
	164	Oxford
Explorer maps	170	Abingdon, Wantage & Vale of White Horse
	180	Oxford

Taxi Services

Place	Name	Telephone numbers
Lechlade	CTs	01367 252575
	Bampton Castle Cars	01993 851007
Carterton	Charlie's Taxis	01993 845253
Faringdon	Stephen Shaw	01367 240804
	Nigel Matson	01367 241121
	Doug Timms	01367 241820
	Shannon Cars	07855 173643
Southmoor	Southmoor Taxis	01865 820984

Car Parking

The following is a list of public car parks close to the Thames Path and does not include on-street parking in villages or towns. Where there are several car parks in a town/city, those closest to the Path have been listed. Unfortunately theft from vehicles parked in the countryside does occasionally occur, so please leave valuables you don't want to carry at home.

Place	Map Grid Reference
Lechlade Riverside, on A361 ¹/2 mile south of Lechlade	SU 211990
Buscot	SU 231977
Radcot Bridge	SU 285995

Toilets

Place	Map Grid Reference
Lechlade Riverside park ♿	SU 211990
Lechlade, St John's Lock	SU 222990
Buscot ♿	SU 231976
Radcot Lock	SP 292002
Rushey Lock	SP 323001

Tourist Information Centres

*Offers accommodation booking service for personal callers during opening hours.

Place	Address/Opening Hours
*Faringdon	The Pump House, 5 Market Place, Faringdon SN7 7HL **T/F:** 01367 242191 www.visitvale.co.uk **Opening hours:** Summer (Easter-Oct 31): Mon-Fri 09:30-16:30; Sat 09:30-13:00 Winter (Nov 1-Easter) Mon-Sat 09:30-13:00
*Witney	26A Market Square, Witney OX28 6BB **T:** 01993 775802 **F:** 01993 709261 witney.vic@westoxon.gov.uk **Opening hours:** Summer: (Apr 1-Oct 31) Mon-Sat 9:30-17:30 Winter: (Nov 1-Mar 31) Mon-Sat 10:00-16:30

BUSCOT

↖N↓ **SU2397** ⊿ **0.4miles (0.6km)**
🚂 **Swindon 11.2miles (18km) PF**
📱 ⊛ ♿WC

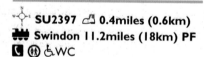

S M T W T F S   S M T W T F S

☆ Buscot Park
T: 01367 240786 **F:** 01367 241744
E: estbuscot@aol.com
www.buscot-park.com

☆ Buscot Village National Trust
Property
T: 01793 762209
E: rebecca.rees@nationaltrust.org.uk
www.nationaltrust.org.uk

Weston Farm   *Closed Xmas Day*

Mr Andrew Woof
Buscot Wick, Faringdon SN7 8DJ
T: 01367 252222 **M:** 07803 937089
F: 01367 252230
E: westonfarmbandb@amserve.co.uk
🛏 2 £55 🛏 1 £55 (£40) ⊘ ♟ ▤
V DRY ♿ ◆◆◆◆ All rooms have
private bathroom facilities.
▐ VisitBritain Silver Award.

KELMSCOTT

 SU2599 **0.3miles (0.5km)**
🚂 **Swindon 14miles (22.5km)** 📞

S M T W T F S   S M T W T F S

Pub: Plough Inn 01367 253543

☆ Kelmscott Manor
T: 01367 252486 **F:** 01367 253754
E: admin@kelmscottmanor.co.uk
www.kelmscottmanor.co.uk

RADCOT

 SU2899 **on path**
🚂 **Swindon 14.9miles (24km)PF** 📞

S M T W T F S   S M T W T F S

Pub: Swan Hotel 01367 810220

Swan Hotel 🏨 ⛺

Mrs Linda Mitchell
Radcot, Bampton OX18 2SX
T: 01367 810220 **M:** 07947 023300
F: 01367 810161
E: swanhotel@swanhotelradcot.co.uk
www.swanhotelradcot.co.uk

👢 1 £45 (£40) 👢 2 £50 🚭 👫
📷 V 🍴 🅿 DRY 🍳 🚗 👢 VISA
Mastercard, Visa, American Express,
Delta.
🛏 For family rooms, add £10 per
additional adult/child.

⛺ 30 £4 🚐 10 £6 📷 🚿 ⚥ 🏪 CG

The Swan Hotel

Tel Mrs Linda Mitchell 01367 810220

The Swan Hotel, dating from the latter part of the 17th century, is a delightful riverside Inn set in beautiful countryside on the banks of the River Thames, whether you are walking on the Thames Path, cruising the river or merely needing a tranquil place to relax.

Homely and comfortable, a warm welcome awaits you. Enjoy al-fresco dining on our riverside decking in summer, or in a cosy restaurant, toasting your toes in front of a blazing log fire in winter.

Comfortable accommodation includes full English Breakfast.

FARINGDON

SU2895 2.8miles (4.5km)
Swindon 12.2miles (19.5km)

Town with full range of services; visit www.faringdon.org for further details. Faringdon has a wide range of accommodation – details from Tourist Information Centre (see section introduction).

☆ Faringdon Folly
T: 01367 240450

CLANFIELD

SP2801 1.8miles (2.9km)
Shipton, but Oxford offers best rail & bus connect 9.9miles (16km) PF

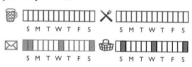

| | S M T W T F S | | S M T W T F S |
| S M T W T F S | | S M T W T F S |

Pubs: Clanfield Tavern 01367 810223 & Plough Hotel 0870 4188031. For further information visit www.clanfield.org

The Plough Hotel Clanfield

Mr Alan Brazier
Bourton Road, Clanfield OX18 2RB
T: 01367 810222
E: bookings@theploughclanfield.co.uk
12 £110 2 £110 1 £55 (£75) 1 £75 Mastercard, Visa, Delta ★★★ All rooms en-suite. For family room, add £25 per child/£55 per adult.

BAMPTON

SP3103 2.2miles (3.6km)
Oxford 18miles (29km) PF
&WC

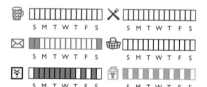

	S M T W T F S		S M T W T F S
S M T W T F S		S M T W T F S
S M T W T F S		S M T W T F S

£ HSBC

For further information on Bampton visit www.bamptonoxon.co.uk

Wheelgate House B&B

Ms Elizabeth Gooddy
Market Square, Bampton OX18 2JH
T: 01993 851151 **M:** 07796 951405
E: wheelgatehouse@hotmail.co.uk
www.wheelgatehouse.co.uk
1 £65 1 £60 (£39) V
Some rooms en-suite.

Clematis

The Trout
at Tadpole Bridge

An 18th Century inn on the banks of the Thames in Oxfordshire.

One of the main reasons to visit is the high standard of cuisine. Daily changing specials with an emphasis on fish, shellfish and local game. Well kept cask ales, mostly from local breweries, with a fine selection of over 120 wines. 6 individually designed, spacious bedrooms with plasma screen TVs and DVD players and luxury toiletries.

Tel: *01367 870382*
Email: *info@troutinn.co.uk*
www.troutinn.co.uk

TADPOLE BRIDGE

SP3300 on path
Oxford 15.5miles (25km)

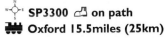
S M T W T F S   S M T W T F S

Pub: Trout Inn 01367 870382

Trout Inn   *Closed Xmas & New Year*

Mr Gareth Pugh
Tadpole Bridge, Buckland Marsh,
Faringdon SN7 8RF
T: 01367 870382 **F:** 01367 870515
E: info@troutinn.co.uk
www.troutinn.co.uk

5 £100 (£70) 1 £130

Mastercard, Visa, Delta ◆◆◆◆ All rooms en-suite

Rushey Lock — *Closed Nov-March*

The Lock Keeper
Tadpole Bridge, Buckland Marsh,
Faringdon SN7 8RF
T: 01367 870218

Shifford Lock — *Closed Oct-Easter*

The Lock Keeper
Chimney, Bampton OX18 2EJ
T: 01367 870247

Informal camping only, by prior arrangement with the Lock Keeper.

BUCKLAND

SU3498 1.5miles (2.4km)
Oxford 14miles (22.5km)PF

S M T W T F S   S M T W T F S

Pub: Lamb 01367 870484

HINTON WALDRIST

SU3899 1.4miles (2.3km)
Oxford 12.8miles (20.5km)

The Stables Ashtree Farm — SC

Mrs Patricia Elliot
Ashtree Farm, Buckland, Faringdon SN7 8PX
T: 01367 870540 **M:** 07971 207188
F: 01367 870541 **E:** info@ashtreefarm.demon.co.uk
www.thestables-ashtreefarm.co.uk
Self-catering unit (with double/twin) from £620 per week.
(min age 9) Various
★★★★★

The Old Rectory

Mr & Mrs Taylor
Hinton Waldrist, Faringdon SN7 8SA
T: 01865 821288 **M:** 07900 826206
F: 01865 821193 **E:** sue@taylor-net.com
www.taylor-net.com/bb
1 £50 1 £55(£40) (min age 10) V DRY ◆◆◆◆ All rooms en-suite

LONGWORTH

 **SU3999** 1.2miles (2km)

Oxford 11.5miles (18.5km)

Pubs: Blue Boar 01865 820494 & Lamb and Flag 01865 820208

1 The Limes

Mrs Sue Hosty
1 The Limes, Church Lane,
Longworth OX13 5DX
T: 01865 821219
E: sue.hosty@virgin.net
2 £55 (£40)
All rooms en-suite

NEWBRIDGE

 **SP4001** on path

Oxford 11.5miles (18.5km)

Pubs: Maybush 01865 300624 & Rose Revived 01865 300221

The Limes

We offer a friendly welcome in a village location, just 1½ miles from the Thames Path. Downstairs accommodation, newly refurbished. En suite with private lounge and garden. Organic food where available. Smoke free rooms. Dogs welcome. Local tavern

Tel: *01865 821219*
Email: *sue.hosty@virgin.net*

Shifford Lock

Section 4

Newbridge to Oxford

The River Thames has grown to a respectable size by the time it leaves Newbridge and is usually pretty well used by a range of boats. The Thames Path along this 14 miles (22km) stretch is still remote and amazingly rural right until the centre of Oxford is reached.

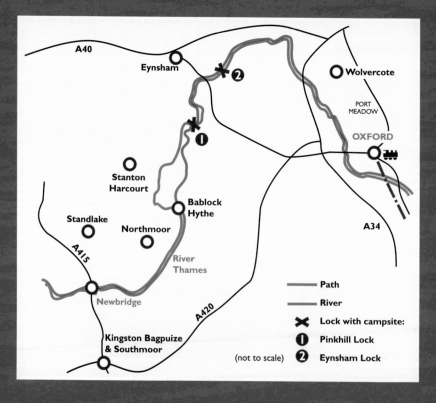

Maps

Landranger maps	164	Oxford
Explorer maps	180	Oxford

Taxi Services

Place	Name	Telephone numbers
Southmoor	Southmoor Taxis	01865 820984
Oxford	City Cars	01865 820984
Oxford	001 Taxis	01865 240000
Oxford	ABC Taxis	01865 770077 or 775577
Oxford	24seven Taxis	01865 423456

Car Parking

The following is a list of public car parks close to the Thames Path and does not include on-street parking in villages or towns. Where there are several car parks in a town/city, those closest to the Path have been listed. Unfortunately theft from vehicles parked in the countryside does occasionally occur, so please leave valuables you don't want to carry at home.

Place	Map Grid Reference
Wolvercote	SP 487095
Oxford, Port Meadow	SP 502074
Oxford City Centre, various	

The High, Oxford

Toilets

Place	Map Grid Reference
Eynsham Lock ♿	SP 445086
Wolvercote ♿	SP 487095
Oxford, various ♿	

Tourist Information Centres

*Offers accommodation booking service for personal callers during opening hours.

Place   **Address/Opening Hours**

*Witney

26A Market Square, Witney OX28 6BB,
T: 01993 775802, **F**: 01993 709261
witney.vic@westoxon.gov.uk
Opening hours:
Summer: (Apr 1-Oct 31) Mon-Sat 9:30-17:30
Winter: (Nov 1-Mar 31) Mon-Sat 10:00-16:30

*Oxford

15-16 Broad Street, Oxford OX1 3AS
T: 01865 726871 **F**: 01865 240261
Opening hours:
Mon-Sat 9:30-17:00; Sun/Bank holidays 10:00-16:00

Newbridge

STANDLAKE

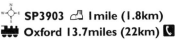 **SP3903** ⌂ 1mile (1.8km)
🚂 Oxford 13.7miles (22km) 📞

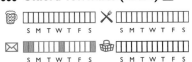
S M T W T F S   S M T W T F S

S M T W T F S   S M T W T F S

Pubs: Black Horse 01865 300307 & Bell
01865 300784

☆ Hardwick Parks Leisure park with
variety of activities available
T: 01865 300501
E: info@hardwickparks.co.uk
www.hardwickparks.co.uk

⚠ **Lincoln Farm Park**   *Closed Nov-Jan*

Mr Stephen Wilders
High Street, Standlake OX29 7RH
T: 01865 300239
E: info@lincolnfarmpark.co.uk
www.lincolnfarmpark.co.uk
⚠ 22 £11 🚐 70 £11 ▨ ⛽ 🚿 ♿
🚾WC ▥ 📞 DRY 🔲 🍴 CG 💳
Mastercard, Visa ★★★★★

⚠ **Hardwick Parks**   *Closed Nov-Mar*

Mrs Nicola Hunt
Downs Road, Standlake OX29 7PZ
T: 01865 300501 **F:** 01865 300037
E: info@hardwickparks.co.uk
www.hardwickparks.co.uk
⚠ 107 £10 🚐 107 £10 ▨ ⛽ 🚿
♿ 🚾WC ▥ 📞 🔲 🍴 CG 💳
Mastercard, Visa, Delta ★★★

KINGSTON BAGPUIZE AND SOUTHMOOR

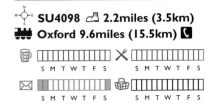 **SU4098** ⌂ 2.2miles (3.5km)
🚂 Oxford 9.6miles (15.5km) 📞

S M T W T F S   S M T W T F S

S M T W T F S   S M T W T F S

Visit www.kbsonline.org.uk for further
details

☆ Kingston Bagpuize House
T: 01865 820259

Fallowfields Country House Hotel Ⓗ

Mrs Peta Lloyd
Faringdon Road, Southmoor with
Kingston Bagpuize OX13 5BH
T: 01865 820416 **F:** 01865 821275
E: stay@fallowfields.com
www.fallowfields.com
🛏 10 £90 🛏 10 £90 (£80) 🛏 2
£120 🚭 ♨ ▨ V ⚲ 🅝 DRY 🔲 👶
💳 Mastercard, Visa, American Express
Delta ◆◆◆◆ All rooms en-suite.
Ⓗ VisitBritain Silver Award

NORTHMOOR

 **SP4202** 🥾 1mile (1.8km)
🚂 **Oxford 14miles (22.5km)** ☎

S M T W T F S   S M T W T F S

Pub: Red Lion 01865 300301

SC **Rectory Farm B&B & Holiday Cottages**

Mrs Mary Anne Florey
Nothmoor, Witney OX29 5SX
T: 01865 300207 **M:** 07974 102198
F: 01865 300559
E: PJ.Florey@farmline.com
www.oxtowns.co.uk/rectoryfarm
🛏 1 £65 🛏 1 £65(£45) 🚭 👫(min
age 14) **V** 🐾 **DRY** 📷 🚗 All rooms
en-suite
♿ B&B closed mid Dec - mid Jan.
Self-catering accommodation ★★★★
open all year and for all ages. Prices
from £300-£400 per week. Prices on
application for short breaks.

BABLOCK HYTHE

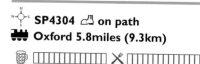 **SP4304** 🥾 on path
🚂 **Oxford 5.8miles (9.3km)**

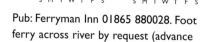

S M T W T F S   S M T W T F S

Pub: Ferryman Inn 01865 880028. Foot
ferry across river by request (advance
warning required), phone 01865 880028

The Ferryman Inn   *closed Xmas* 🏨 ⛺

Mr Peter Kelland
Bablock Hythe, Northmoor OX29 5AT
T: 01865 880028
🛏 3 £65 🛏 2 £65 (£35) 🛏 1 £75
🚭 👫 **V** 🐾 🌙 **DRY** ◆◆◆Some rooms
en-suite.
⛺ 6 £5 🚐 5 £10 🚿 🚽 ♿ **DRY**CG

STANTON HARCOURT

 **SP4105** 🥾 0.9miles (1.5km)
🚂 **Oxford 8.5miles (13.6km)** ☎

📧 S M T W T F S   🧺 S M T W T F S

Pubs: Fox 01865 881551 & Harcourt
Arms 01865 881931

Purple loosestrife

EYNSHAM

 **SP4309** 🥾 **0.9miles (1.5km)**
🚂 **Coombe 4.7miles (7.5km)**

Small town with full range of services; visit www.eynsham.org for further details

Pinkhill Lock   *Closed Oct-March*

The Lock Keeper
Eynsham OX8 1JH
T: 01865 881452
🏕 10 🚰 ⓦ 🗓

Eynsham Lock

The Lock Keeper
Swinford Bridge, Eynsham OX8 1BY
T: 01865 881324
🏕 10 🚰 ⓦ 🗓

WOLVERCOTE

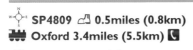 **SP4809** 🥾 **0.5miles (0.8km)**
🚂 **Oxford 3.4miles (5.5km)** 📞

OXFORD

 **SP5106** 🥾 **on path**
🚂 **Oxford**

City with full range of services, museums, colleges and other attractions. Visit www.visitoxford.org for further details. Oxford has a wide range of accommodation – details from Tourist Information Centre (see section introduction).

Oxford YHA

Mr Jonathan Brewer
2A Botley Road, Oxford OX2 0AB
T: 01865 727275 **F:** 01865 251182
E: oxford@yha.org.uk
www.yha.org.uk
🛏 9 £49 🛏 12 £52 (£35) ⊘ 🚻 ♿
V 🔥 🟢 DRY ⓞ 💳 Visa, Mastercard, Delta ★★★★ All rooms en-suite
🛏 Also dormitory from £18/adult

Oxford Camping & Caravanning Site

The Manager
426 Abingdon Road, Oxford OX1 4XN
T: 01865 244088 www.
campingandcaravanningclub.co.uk
🏕 43 £5 🚐 42 £6 📶 🚰 🚰 ⓦ 🗓
DRY ⓞ CG

Section 5

Oxford to Abingdon

This relatively short section of 10 miles (16km) is still essentially rural once the Thames Path has left the centre of Oxford striking south. Once beyond Sandford-on-Thames there are no settlements close by until Abingdon is reached.

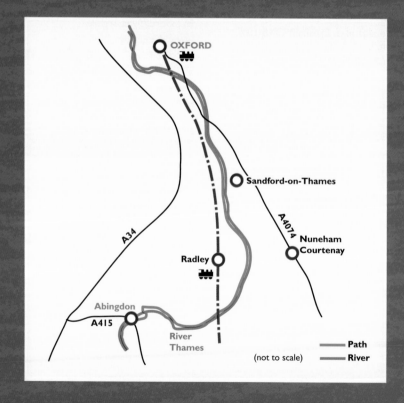

Maps

Landranger maps	164	Oxford
Explorer maps	180	Oxford
	170	Abingdon, Wantage & Vale of White Horse

Taxi Services

Place	Name	Telephone numbers
Oxford	City Cars	01865 820984
Oxford	001 Taxis	01865 240000
Oxford	ABC Taxis	01865 770077 or 775577
Oxford	24seven Taxis	01865 423456
Radley	Rural Car Service	0800 0743494
Abingdon	Auto Taxis	01235 527711 or 520283
Abingdon	Toots Taxis	01235 555599
Abingdon	Phil's Taxis	01235 522555
Abingdon	Vargan Taxis	01235 559606
Abingdon	Streamline Taxis	01235 521501

Car Parking

The following is a list of public car parks close to the Thames Path and does not include on-street parking in villages or towns. Where there are several car parks in a town, those closest to the Path have been listed. Unfortunately theft from vehicles parked in the countryside does occasionally occur, so please leave valuables you don't want to carry at home.

Place	Map Grid Reference
Oxford, Port Meadow	SP 502074
Oxford City Centre, various	
Abingdon, Rye Farm, on A415 south of Abingdon Bridge	SU 501967
Abingdon, Hales Meadow car park, downstream side of bridge	SU 500967

Toilets

Place	Map Grid Reference
Oxford, various ♿	
Abingdon Lock ♿	SU 506971
Abingdon, Hales Meadow car park, downstream side of bridge ♿	SU 500967

Tourist Information Centres

* Offers accommodation booking service for personal callers during opening hours.

Place	Address/Opening Hours
*Oxford	15-16 Broad Street, Oxford OX1 3AS **T**: 01865 726871 **F**: 01865 240261 **Opening hours:** Mon-Sat 9:30-17:00; Sun/Bank holidays 10:00-16:00
*Abingdon	Abingdon Information Point, Abingdon Town Council, Old Abbey House, Abbey Close, Abingdon OX14 3JD **T**: 01235 522711 **F**: 01235 533112 info@abingdon.gov.uk www.visitvale.co.uk **Opening hours:** Summer (1 June-30 Sept) Mon-Sat 10:00-16:00 Winter (1 Oct-31 May) Mon-Sat 10:00-15:00

SANDFORD-ON-THAMES

SP5301 on path
Oxford 4.7miles (7.5km)

S M T W T F S   S M T W T F S

NUNEHAM COURTENAY

SU5599 2.1miles (3.5km)
Oxford 6.5miles (10.5km)

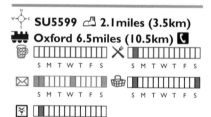

S M T W T F S   S M T W T F S

S M T W T F S   S M T W T F S

S M T W T F S

Pub: Harcourt Arms 01865 340202.

☆ Harcourt Arboretum, the oldest arboretum in the country
T: 01865 343501

Wild rose

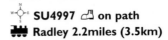

The Old Bakery B&B

Mrs Jill Addison
Nuneham Courtenay OX44 9NX
T/ F: 01235 537538
E: addisonjill@hotmail.co.uk
www.theoldbakery-oxford.com
🛏 1 £75 🛏 1 £75 🛏 1 £105
(£50) ⛄ 📺V 🎵 **DRY** 🚗 **VISA**
Mastercard, Visa. All rooms en-suite

RADLEY

🧭 **SP5299** 👣 **0.9miles (1.5km)**
🚂 **Radley** 📞

Pub: Bowyer Arms 01235 523452

Hollies Guest House

Mr Brian Holloway
8 New Road, Radley OX14 3AP
T: 01235 529552
E: lajardiere@tiscali.co.uk
🛏 2 £50 (£25) 🚭 ⛄ V 🎵 🌑 🐾
DRY 🚗

ABINGDON

🧭 **SU4997** 👣 **on path**
🚂 **Radley 2.2miles (3.5km)**

Town with full range of services, visit
www.abingdon.gov.uk for further
details. Abingdon has a wide range of
accommodation – details from Tourist
Information Centre (see section
introduction). However the one listed
here particularly welcomes Thames
Path walkers.

☆ Kingcraft Day Boats **T:** 01235
521125

☆ Abingdon Abbey **T:** 01235 525339

☆ Abingdon Museum **T:** 01235
523703

Kingfisher Barn   SC

Miss Sarah Jefferies
Rye Farm, Abingdon OX14 3NN
T/F: 01235 537538
E: info@kingfisherbarn.com
www.kingfisherbarn.com
🛏 2 £75 🛏 8 £75 🛏 2 £85
(£57) 🛏 10 £57 🚭 ⛄ ♿ 🐾 **DRY**
🐾 **🚋** Mastercard, Visa, American
Express, Delta Switch, ★★★★
Some rooms en-suite
🏠 Self-catering accommodation also
available from £319

Crab apple

Section 6

Abingdon to Wallingford

It is during this 13½ miles (22km) section that settlements start to become more frequent, for as well as starting and finishing in historic towns, several villages are encountered on or close to the Thames Path. However, in between the countryside remains generally quiet.

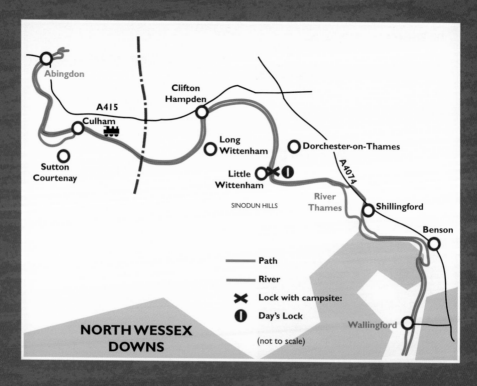

Maps

Landranger maps	164	Oxford
	175	Reading & Windsor
Explorer maps	180	Oxford

Taxi Services

Place	Name	Telephone numbers
Abingdon	Auto Taxis	01235 527711 or 520283
Abingdon	Toots Taxis	01235 555599
Abingdon	Phil's Taxis	01235 522555
Abingdon	Vargan Taxis	01235 559606
Abingdon	Streamline Taxis	01235 521501
Wallingford	Hills Taxis	01491 837022
Wallingford	Rural Car Service	0800 0743494

Car Parking

The following is a list of public car parks close to the Thames Path and does not include on-street parking in villages or towns. Where there are several car parks in a town, those closest to the Path have been listed. Unfortunately theft from vehicles parked in the countryside does occasionally occur, so please leave valuables you don't want to carry at home.

Place	Map Grid Reference
Abingdon, Rye Farm, on A415 south of Abingdon Bridge	SU 501967
Abingdon, Hales Meadow car park, downstream side of bridge	SU 500967
Culham Lock	SU 507949
Clifton Hampden bridge, south of river opposite Barley Mow pub	SU 548953
Wallingford Riverside, east of the river	SU 612895

Toilets

Place	Map Grid Reference
Abingdon Lock ♿	SU 506971
Abingdon, Hales Meadow car park, downstream side of bridge ♿	SU 500967
Culham Lock	SU 507949
Wallingford, Cattle Market car park, Wood Street ♿	SU 608893

Tourist Information Centres

* Offers accommodation booking service for personal callers during opening hours.

Place	Address/Opening Hours
*Abingdon	Abingdon Information Point, Abingdon Town Council, Old Abbey House, Abbey Close, Abingdon OX14 3JD
	T: 01235 522711 **F:** 01235 533112
	info@abingdon.gov.uk
	www.visitvale.co.uk
	Opening hours:
	Summer (1 June-30 Sept) Mon-Sat 10:00-16:00
	Winter (1 Oct-31 May) Mon-Sat 10:00-15:00
*Wallingford	Town Hall, Market Place, Wallingford OX10 0EG.
	T: 01491 826972 **F:** 01491 825844
	Opening hours:
	All year: Mon-Sat 09:30-17:00

Abingdon

CULHAM

SU5095 🥾 **on path**
🚂 **Culham 1.6miles (2.5km) PF** 📞

🍺 |||||||||||| ✕ ||||||||||||
　S M T W T F S　　S M T W T F S

Pubs: Lion 01235 520327 & Waggon and Horses 01235 525012

SUTTON COURTENAY

SU5093 🥾 **0.9miles (1.5km)**
🚂 **Didcot 3.4miles (5.5km) PF** 📞

🍺 |||||||||||| ✕ ||||||||||||
　S M T W T F S　　S M T W T F S

✉ |||||||||||| 🧺 ||||||||||||
　S M T W T F S　　S M T W T F S

Appletree Cottage B&B

Mr & Mrs Worrell
5 Appletree Cottage, Appleford Road,
Sutton Courtenay OX14 4NG
T: 01235 848071
E: b&b@appletreecottage-bb.co.uk
🛏 1 £42 🛏 2 £42 🛏 1 £55
(£38) 🛏 3 £30 (£30) 🚫 🍴 ♿ 📷V
DRY All rooms en-suite

Bekynton House　　　*Closed Xmas*

Ms Sue Cornwall
7 The Green, Sutton Courtenay
OX14 4AE
T: 01235 848888 **M:** 07968 776691
E: susancornwall@aol.com
www.a1tourism.com/uk/bekynton.html
🛏 1 £70 🛏 2 £70 (£35) 🛏 1 £35
🚫 🍴 V 🦺 **DRY** 📷 ♿Some rooms
en-suite

The Fish　　　INN

Mrs Marilyn England
4 Appleford Road, Sutton Courtenay,
Abingdon OX14 4NQ
T: 01235 848242 **F:** 01235 848014
E: info@thefish.uk.com
www.thefish.uk.com
🛏 1 £50 🛏 2 £50 (£40) 🚫
🍴(minimum 7) ♿ 📷V 🦺 🌙 **DRY** 📷
♿ **VISA** Mastercard, Visa

CLIFTON HAMPDEN

SU5495 🥾 **on path**
🚂 **Culham 1.1miles (1.8km)** 📞

🍺 |||||||||||| ✕ ||||||||||||
　S M T W T F S　　S M T W T F S

✉ |||||||||||| 🧺 ||||||||||||
　S M T W T F S　　S M T W T F S

Pubs: Plough Inn 01865 407136 &
Barley Mow 01865 407847

Bridge House Caravan Site
Closed Nov-March

Miss E Gower
Bridge House, Clifton Hampden,
Abingdon OX14 3EH
T: 01865 407725
🏕 20 £5 🚐 20 £10 ▢ ▢ ▢ ▢ ▢

The Plough Inn

Mrs Olwyn Stilwell
Abingdon Road, Clifton Hampden,
Abingdon OX14 3EG
T: 01865 407811 **F:** 01865 407136
E: admin@ploughinns.co.uk
www.ploughinns.co.uk
🛏 6 £75 🛏 1 £90 *(£75)* 🛏 6
£75 ▢ ▢ V ▢ ▢ **DRY** ▢ ▢ **VISA**
Mastercard, Visa, Switch, Solo. All rooms
en-suite

LONG WITTENHAM

✦ **SU5493** 🚶 1.6miles (2.5km)
🚂 Culham 2.4miles (3.8km)

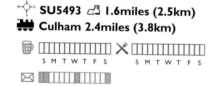
S M T W T F S   S M T W T F S

S M T W T F S

Pubs: Plough 01865 407738 & Vine Inn
01865 407832.

☆ Pendon Museum of Miniature
Landscape and Transport - limited
opening **T:** 01865 407365
www.pendonmuseum.com

Witta's Ham Cottage *Closed Xmas*

Mrs Jill Mellor
High Street, Long Wittenham, Abingdon
OX14 4QH
T: 01865 407686 **F:** 01865 407469
E: bandb@wittenham.com
🛏 1 £56 🛏 1 £56 *(£38)* 🛏 1 £36
▢ ▢ (min age 6) V ▢ **DRY** ▢ ▢ ▢
◆◆◆◆
▪ VisitBritain Silver Award

The Grange

Mr Graham Neil
Long Wittenham, Abingdon OX14 4QH
T: 01865 407808 **M:** 07831 581544
F: 01865 407939
E: grahamneil@talk21.com
www.smoothhound.co.uk/hotels/grange5.html
🛏 2 £55 🛏 2 £55 *(£40)* ▢ ▢
(min age 8) ▢ V ▢ **DRY** ▢ ▢ ▢
★★★ Some rooms en-suite

LITTLE WITTENHAM

✦ **SU5693** 🚶 0.3miles (0.5km)
🚂 Culham 3.4miles (5.5km) 📞

☆ Little Wittenham Nature Reserve
T: 01865 407792 **F:** 01865 407131
E: admin@northmoortrust.co.uk
www.northmoortrust.co.uk

Day's Lock   Closed Oct-Easter

The Lock Keeper
Little Wittenham, Abingdon OX14 4RD
T: 01865 407768
🏕 5 ▢ ▢ ▢

DORCHESTER-ON-THAMES

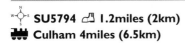 **SU5794** ⛺ **1.2miles (2km)**
🚉 **Culham 4miles (6.5km)**

Small town with range of services; visit
www.dorchester-on-thames.co.uk for
further details

☆ Dorchester Abbey & Museum
T: 01865 340007
E: enquiries@dorchester-abbey.org.uk
www.dorchester-abbey.org.uk

🏠 **The White Hart Hotel**

Mr Sean Harris
High Street, Dorchester-on-Thames
OX10 7HN
T: 01865 340074 **F:** 01865 341082
E: whitehart@oxfordshire-hotels.co.uk
www.oxfordshire-hotels.co.uk
🛏 19 £95 🛏 5 £95 (£85) 🛏
2 £105 🛏 2 £75 🚫 👫 ♿ 📺 V 🔥
🌙 **DRY** 🅾 🐕 📼 Mastercard, Visa,
American Express ★★★ All rooms
en-suite

SHILLINGFORD

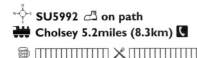 **SU5992** ⛺ **on path**
🚉 **Cholsey 5.2miles (8.3km)** 📞

Pubs: Kingfisher Inn 01865 858595 and
Shillingford Bridge Hotel 01865 858567

The Kingfisher Inn 🏨

Mr Alexis Somarakis
27 Henley Road, Shillingford OX10 7EL
T: 01865 858595
E: guestrooms@kingfisher-inn.co.uk
www.kingfisher-inn.co.uk
🛏 5 £79 🛏 1 £79 (£62) 🛏 1 £62
🚫 👫 V 🔥 🌙 **DRY** 🐕 📼 Mastercard,
Visa, Delta ◆◆◆◆ All rooms en-suite

Marsh House

Mrs Patricia Nickson
Court Drive, Shillingford OX10 7ER
T: 01865 858496 **M:** 07702 454837
F: 01865 858590
E: marsh.house@talk21.com
www.marshhousebandb.co.uk
🛏 1 £60 🛏 1 £60 (£40) 🛏 1 £75
🛏 1 £35 🚫 👫 (min age 8) V 🔥 **DRY**
🐕 ◆◆◆ All rooms en-suite

Shillingford Bridge Hotel 🏠

Mrs Fender
Shillingford Hill, Wallingford OX10 8LZ
T: 01865 858567 **F:** 01865 858636
www.shillingfordbridgehotel.com
🛏 22 £125 🛏 8 £125 🛏 1 £90
👫 ♿ 📺 V 🔥 🌙 **DRY** 🅾 🐕 📼
Mastercard, Visa, American Express,
Delta ★★★ All rooms en-suite

Bridge House

Mrs RA Mader-Grayson
72 Wallingford Road, Shillingford OX10 7EU
T: 01865 858251
E: house@bridge-house.org.uk
www.bridge-house.org.uk
🛏 2 £50 (£35) 🚭 ♀♂ 🚗 V 🔥 🌐
DRY 🍽 🚗 🧑‍🦯 All rooms en-suite
⛺ 10 £5 🚐 5 £6 🔌 DRY 🍽 ⚓ ⚒ 🅿 📱
🎮 CG
🅷 Tea Rooms also on site. Camping closed Oct-Easter

BENSON

⊹ SU6191 🥾 on path
🚂 Cholsey 5.1 miles (8.2km) P F
📞 ⚒

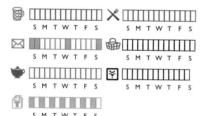

£ Cash machine at service station ⚛
Pubs: Crown Inn 01491 838247 & Three Horseshoes 01491 838242

☆ Veteran Cycles - by appointment only
T: 01491 838414

Brookside

Mrs Jill Folley
Brook Street, Benson OX10 6LJ
T/F: 01491 838289 **M:** 07979 813302
E: clive@clivefolley.wanadoo.co.uk
🛏 1 £60 (£40) 🛏 1 £90 ♀♂ 🚗 V
DRY 🍽 🚗 🧑‍🦯 ◆◆◆◆ All rooms
en-suite

Fyfield Manor

Mrs Brown
Benson OX10 6HA
T: 01491 835184 **M:** 07779 722202
F: 01491 825635
E: chris_fyfield@hotmail.co.uk
www.fyfieldmanor.co.uk
🛏 1 £65 🛏 1 £65 (£45) 🚭 ♀♂
(min age 10) V 🔥 DRY ★★★★ All
rooms en-suite
🅷 VisitBritain Silver Award. Family room available, price on application. Single occupancy weekdays only.

Benson Waterfront *Closed Nov-March* ⛺

Mr B Dandridge
Benson OX10 6SJ
T: 01491 838304 **F:** 01491 836738
E: camping@bensonwaterfront.com
www.bensonwaterfront.com
⛺ 6 £12 🚐 16 £14 🔌 ⚓ ⚒ ⚒
♿WC 📱 🍽 🎮 CG 💳 Mastercard, Visa, Delta

WALLINGFORD

SU6089 on path
Cholsey 2.9miles (4.7km)
Town with full range of services,
visit www.wallingford.org for further
details. Wallingford has a wide range
of accommodation – details from
Tourist Information Centre (see
section introduction). However, the
accommodation providers listed here
particularly welcome Thames Path
walkers.

☆ Wallingford Museum
T: 01491 835065
www.wallingford.org

☆ Wallingford Castle - limited opening
hours in winter

The George Hotel

Mr O Round-Turner
High Street, Wallingford OX10 0BS
T: 01491 836665 **F:** 01491 825359
E: info@george-hotel-wallingford.com
www.george-hotel-wallingford.com
9 £98 21 £98 (£90) 1
£105 8 £65 ✝↑ & V ⚕ Ⓢ DRY ⓞ
Mastercard, Visa, American Express,
Delta ★★★ All rooms en-suite and
some non-smoking

52 Blackstone Road

Mrs Enid Barnard
52 Blackstone Road, Wallingford OX10
8JL
T: 01491 839339
E: enid.barnard@mediummail.co.uk
1 £35 (£25) 1 £20 Ⓢ ⚑ V
DRY

The Old School House

Mrs Carolyn Booth
23 Castle Street, Wallingford OX10
8DW
T: 01491 839571 **M:** 07900 225167
F: 01491 826489
E: bristow.carolyn@googlemail.com
2 £55 Ⓢ ✝↑ V ⚕ DRY ⓞ All
rooms en-suite

The Studio

Mrs P Smith
85 Wantage Road, Wallingford OX10
0LT
T: 01491 837277 **F:** 01491 825036
E: pam@prufit.co.uk
www.wallingfordbandb.co.uk
1 £50 1 £50 (£35) 1 £25
Ⓢ ✝↑ & V ⚕ DRY ⓞ 🚗 All
rooms en-suite

Section

7

Wallingford to Tilehurst

These 15 miles (24km) of the Thames Path finishing on the
outskirts of Reading provide contrasting landscapes and some
lovely settlements. Firstly there's open countryside with wide
views but before long the River Thames is squeezed between
hills as it passes through the Goring Gap with the wooded
Chilterns as a backdrop.

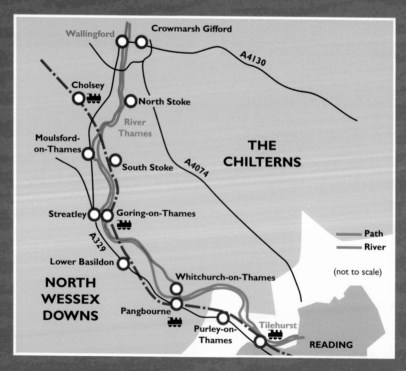

Maps

Landranger maps	175	Reading & Windsor
	174	Newbury & Wantage
Explorer maps	171	Chiltern Hills West

Taxi Services

Place	Name	Telephone numbers
Wallingford	Hills Taxis	01491 837022
Wallingford	Rural Car Service	0800 0743494
Goring-on-Thames	Golden Taxis	01491 871111
Goring-on-Thames	Murdock Taxis	01491 872029

Car Parks

The following is a list of public car parks close to the Thames Path and does not include on-street parking in villages or towns. Where there are several car parks in a town, those closest to the Path have been listed. Unfortunately theft from vehicles parked in the countryside does occasionally occur, so please leave valuables you don't want to carry at home.

Place	Map Grid Reference
Wallingford Riverside, east of the river	SU 612895
Goring-on-Thames	SU 599807
Pangbourne, south side of bridge	SU 636767

Toilets

Place	Map Grid Reference
Wallingford, Cattle Market car park, Wood Street ♿	SU 608893
Cleeve Lock, upstream of Goring-on-Thames ♿	SU 601818
Goring-on-Thames car park ♿	SU 599807
Pangbourne, River Meadow ♿	SU 636767

Tourist Information Centres

* Offers accommodation booking service for personal callers during opening hours.

Place	Address/Opening Hours
*Wallingford	Town Hall, Market Place, Wallingford OX10 0EG **T:** 01491 826972 **F:** 01491 825844 **Opening hours:** All year: Mon-Sat 09:30-17:00
*Reading	Church House, Chain Street, Reading RG1 2HX **T:** 0118 956 6226 **F:** 0118 939 9885 www.readingtourism.org.uk **Opening hours:** All year: Mon, Tue, Thurs, Fri 09:30-17:00; Wed 10:00-17:00, Sat 09:30-16:00

CROWMARSH GIFFORD

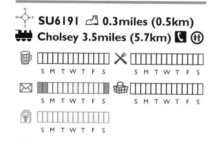

SU6191 0.3miles (0.5km)
Cholsey 3.5miles (5.7km)

	S M T W T F S		S M T W T F S

Pubs: Queen's Head 01491 839857 &
Bell Inn (Hungry Horse) 01491 835324.

B&B at Little Gables

Mrs Jill Reeves
166 Crowmarsh Hill, Wallingford OX10 8BG

T: 01491 837834 **M:** 07860 148882
F: 01491 834426
E: jill@stayingaway.com
www.stayingaway.com

 | £60 | £60 (£50) |
£75 | £45 ⊗ ♥♥ ♿ V ⚠ DRY

★★★★ Some rooms en-suite
⊞ Three rooms in total, can be made into double/twin/family/single room upon request

B&B at Little Gables

A warm welcome is waiting for you. Clean, well furnished rooms with ensuite or private bathrooms. Colour TV, DVD. Garden seating area, off-road parking, packed lunch.

Tel: 01491 837834
Fax: 01491 834426
Email: jill@stayingaway.com
www.stayingaway.com

Riverside Park & Pools
closed Oct–early April

Mr Jeremy Mayo
The Street, Crowmarsh Gifford,
Wallingford OX10 8EB
T: 01491 835232
E: enquiries@soll-leisure.co.uk
www.soll-leisure.co.uk
18 £11 18 £11
WC

Bridge Villa Camping & Caravan Park
Closed Jan

Mr Andrew Townsend
The Street, Crowmarsh Gifford,
Wallingford OX10 8HB
T: 01491 836860 M: 07801 274116
F: 01491 836793
E: bridge.villa@btinternet.com
www.tiscover.co.uk/bridge-villa
55 £9 56 £14
WC CG
Mastercard, Visa, Delta

NORTH STOKE

SU6086 1.9miles (2.7km)
Goring and Streatley 4miles (6.6km)

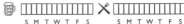
S M T W T F S   S M T W T F S

Pub: Springs Hotel 01491 836687

The Springs Hotel & Golf Club

Mr George Briffa
Wallingford Road, North Stoke
OX10 6BE
T: 01491 836687 F: 01491 836877 E: info@thespringshotel.com
www.thespringshotel.com
21 £110 8 £110 (£95)
3 £135
Mastercard, Visa, American Express, Delta ★★★ All rooms en-suite

CHOLSEY

 **SU5886** 🥾 **0.9miles (1.5km)**
🚃 **Cholsey** 📞

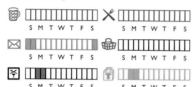

Pubs: Morning Star 01491 651413 &
Red Lion 01491 651295

☆ Cholsey and Wallingford Railway
T: 01491 835067

The Well Cottage

Mrs Joanna Alexander
Caps Lane, Cholsey OX10 9HQ
T: 01491 651959 **M:** 07887 958920
F: 01491 651675
E: joanna@thewellcottage.com
www.thewellcottage.com
🛏 2 £40 ♥♥ ♿ 🖼 **V** ◆◆◆ All
rooms en-suite

33 Ilges Road   *Closed Xmas & New Year*

Mrs Hazel Jensen
Cholsey OX10 9NX
T: 01491 651974
🛏 1 £40 (£23) 🛏 1 £20 🚭 **V** **DRY**

MOULSFORD-ON-THAMES

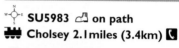 **SU5983** 🥾 **on path**
🚃 **Cholsey 2.1miles (3.4km)** 📞

Pub: Beetle & Wedge Hotel 01491
651381

The Beetle & Wedge Boathouse
Closed Xmas & New Year

Miss Stephanie Hicks
Ferry Lane, Moulsford OX10 9JF
T: 01491 651381 **F:** 01491 651376 **E:**
boathouse@beetleandwedge.co.uk
www.beetleandwedge.co.uk
🛏 1 £90 (£75) 🚭 ♥♥ **V** ⚓ ◑ **DRY**
▣ 🐕 *VISA* Mastercard, Visa, American
Express, Delta. Room is en-suite
🛏 Double room can be a twin room if
required

SOUTH STOKE

 **SU6083** 🥾 **2.6miles (4.2km)**
🚃 **Goring 2.3miles (3.7km)**

Pub: Perch and Pike 01491 872415

The Oak Barn

Mrs Vanessa Guiver
The Old Post Office, The Street, South
Stoke RG8 0JS
T: 01491 871872 **T:** 01491 871873
E: vanessa.guiver@btinternet.com
🛏 1 £70 (£40) ⊗ ♯ V 🔥 ◐ DRY
⊙ 👢 Room is en-suite
❚ Apartment accommodation; cot and
extra bed available upon request.

STREATLEY

⊕ **SU5980** ◁ **on path**
🚂 **Goring and Streatly 0.7miles**
(1.2km) ☎

S M T W T F S   S M T W T F S

Pubs: Bull at Streatley 01491 872392 &
Swan Diplomat Hotel 01491 878800
Most facilities available nearby at
Goring. For further information visit
www.streatley-on-thames.co.uk

Ⓗ The Swan at Streatley

Mr Karl Bentely
Streatley RG8 9HR
T: 01491 878800
E: sales@swan-at-streatley.co.uk
www.swanatstreatley.co.uk
🛏 27 £105 🛏 9 £105 (£90)
🛏 3 £135 🛏 8 £80 ♯ 🚹 ⑤ V 🔥
◐ ⊙ 👢 VISA Mastercard, Visa, American
Express, Delta ★★★★ All rooms en-
suite

Streatley YHA

Mr Nick Crivich
Reading Road, Streatley RG8 9JJ
T: 01491 872278 **F:** 01491 873056
E: streatley@yha.org.uk
www.yhastreatley.org.uk
🛏 2 £40 (£30) 🛏 8 £56
⊗ ♯ V 🔥 ◐ DRY VISA Visa,
Mastercard, Delta ★★★ Some rooms
en-suite
❚ Self-catering from £15.50. Check for
details of seasonal opening.

3 Icknield Cottages

Mr & Mrs J Brodie
High Street, Streatley RG8 9JA
T: 01491 875152 **F:** 01491 875650
🛏 1 £30 ⊗ V DRY ⊙
❚ Private bathroom available

Ridgeways Cottage

Mr John Hardwick
Wantage Road, Streatley RG8 9LA
T: 01491 874112 **M:** 07787 780304
E: j.hardwick@virgin.net
http://freespace.virgin.net/j.hardwick/
index.htm
🛏 1 £50 (£50) ⊗ ♯ 🚹 📷 All
rooms en-suite
❚ Room is self-catering

Stable Cottages *Closed Xmas & New Year*

Mrs Diana Fenton
Streatley RG8 9JX
T: 01491 874408
🛏 1 £50 (£25) 🛏 1 £25 ⊗ �(min age 8) **V** 🚶 **DRY** 🗇 🚶

GORING-ON-THAMES

⊹ **SU6082** 🥾 on path
🚂 **Goring and Streatley**

Small town with range of services

☆ Goring Gap
www.goring-gap.co.uk

3 Lycroft Close

Mrs Frances Thompson
Goring-on-Thames RG8 0AT
T: 01491 873052
E: frances@lycroft.fsnet.co.uk
🛏 1 £50 (£25) 🛏 1 £25 ⊗ ♾ 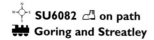 **V** 🚶 **DRY** 🗇 🚗 🚶

Melrose Cottage

Mrs Rosemary Howarth
36 Milldown Road, Goring-on-Thames RG8 0BD
T: 01491 873040 **M:** 07798 663897
E: melrose@fsmail.net
🛏 2 £50 (£30) 🛏 1 £30 **V** 🚶 ⊘ **DRY** 🗇 🚗 🚶

Northview House

Mrs I Sheppard
Farm Road, Goring-on-Thames RG8 0AA
T: 01491 872184 **E:** hi@goring-on-thames.freeserve.co.uk
🛏 2 £50 🛏 1 £50 (£30) 🛏 1 £65
⊗ ♾ 📺 **V** 🚶 **DRY** 🗇

The Queen's Arms 🏨

Mrs Lynn McAuliffe
Reading Road, Goring-on-Thames RG8 0ER
T: 01491 872825 **M:** 07821 544699
E: queensarms_goring@fsmail.net
🛏 1 £60 🛏 1 £60 (£45) 🛏 1 £75
🛏 1 £30 ⊗ ♾ (min age 12) **V** 🚶 🌙

LOWER BASILDON

⊹ **SU6178** 🥾 2.1miles (3.3km)
🚂 **Pangbourne 2.1miles (3.3km)** ☎

S M T W T F S   S M T W T F S

Pub: Crown 01491 671262

☆ Basildon Park - National Trust property
T: 0118 984 3040
E: basildonpark@ntrust.org.uk
www.nationaltrust.org.uk

WHITCHURCH-ON-THAMES

 SU6377 on path
Pangbourne 0.6miles (1km)

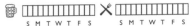
S M T W T F S   S M T W T F S

Pubs: Greyhound 0118 9842160
& Ferryboat 0118 984 2161. For
further information visit www.
whitchurchonthames.com

PANGBOURNE

 SU6376 on path
Pangbourne

Small town with range of services; visit
www.pangbourne-on-thames.com for
further details

☆ Beale Park
T: 0118 9845172 **F:** 0118 9845171
E: bealepark@bun.com
www.bealepark.co.uk

PURLEY-ON-THAMES

 SU6676 on path
Tilehurst 0.6miles (1km)

S M T W T F S   S M T W T F S

Herons Watch *Closed Xmas & New Year*

Mr & Mrs D Jones
68 Wintringham Way, Purley-on-Thames
RG8 8BG
T: 0118 9452291 **M:** 07801 343752
F: 0118 9452093
E: specialeffects@btconnect.com
www.heronswatch.co.uk
 1 £70 V DRY VISA Visa,
Mastercard, American Express, JCB.
Room is en-suite

TILEHURST

 SU6674 on path
Tilehurst

Close to range of services in Reading.
For further information visit www.
tilehurst.net

Firtrees

Mrs T Reed
2 Cotswold Way, Tilehurst RG31 6SH
T: 0118 9413286 **M:** 07900 713184
1 £45 (£30) 2 £25 (min
age 7) V DRY

18 Partridge Drive

Mrs V Wyatt
Tilehurst RG31 4SX
T: 0118 9625419 **M:** 07909 550302
 1 £50 (£30) 2 £25 V
DRY

Section 8

Tilehurst to Henley-on-Thames

Once Reading is left behind this 12 miles (20km) section enjoys a landscape of gentle wooded hills, fine houses and, of course, the ever-widening River Thames. There are also several pleasant settlements en route for refreshments.

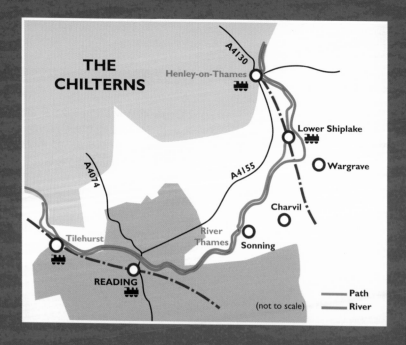

Maps

Landranger maps	175	Reading & Windsor
Explorer maps	171	Chiltern Hills West

Taxi Services

Place	Name	Telephone numbers
Reading	Theale Taxis	0118 9302345
Reading	Thames Valley Taxis Ltd	0118 9484848
Reading	Just Cars	0118 9500400
Reading	Premier Cars	0118 9500500
Sonning	Woodley	0800 654321
Sonning	Top Cars	0118 9442222
Henley	Chiltern Taxis	01491 578899
Henley	County Cars	01491 579696
Henley	Harris Taxis	01491 577036
Henley	Talbot Taxis	01491 574000

Car Parks

The following is a list of public car parks close to the Thames Path and does not include on-street parking in villages or towns. Where there are several car parks in a town, those closest to the Path have been listed. Unfortunately theft from vehicles parked in the countryside does occasionally occur, so please leave valuables you don't want to carry at home.

Place	Map Grid Reference
Reading, various including King's Meadow Road	
Henley-on-Thames, Mill Lane	SU 771817
Henley-on-Thames, Mill Meadows	SU 766822

Toilets

Place	Map Grid Reference
Reading, various ♿	
Sonning Lock	SU 753755
Shiplake Lock	SU 776787
Henley-on-Thames, Mill Meadows ♿	SU 766822

Tourist Information Centres

* Offers accommodation booking service for personal callers during opening hours.

Place	Address/Opening Hours
*Reading	Church House, Chain Street, Reading RG1 2HX **T**: 0118 956 6226 **F**: 0118 939 9885 www.readingtourism.org.uk **Opening hours:** All year: Mon, Tue, Thurs, Fri 09:30-17:00; Wed 10:00-17:00, Sat 09:30-16:00
*Henley-on-Thames	King's Arms Barn, Kings Road, Henley-on-Thames RG9 2DG **T**: 01491 578034 **F**: 01491 411766 **E**: henleyvic@frenchjones.co.uk www.visithenley-on-thames.co.uk **Opening hours:** Summer: (Mar 31-Sep 30) daily 10:00-17:00 Winter: (Oct 1-Mar 31) daily 10:00-16:00

READING

SU7173 **on path**

Reading

Large town with full range of services. Visit www.readingtourism.org.uk for further details. Reading has a wide range of accommodation – details from Tourist Information Centre (see section introduction).

SONNING

SU7675 **on path**

Twyford 2.8miles (4.5km)

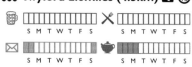

Pubs: Bull Inn 0118 9693901 & Great House 0118 969 2277

The Bull Inn Hotel

Mrs Christine Mason
High Street, Sonning RG4 6UP
T: 0118 9693901 **M:** 07889 331860
F: 0118 9697188
E: dennis@dennismason.com
www.fullers.co.uk
4 £95 1 £125 V
Mastercard, Visa, American
Express, Delta ★★★★
All rooms en-suite.
VisitBritain Silver Award.

The Great House at Sonning

Mrs Julie Rae
Thames Street, Sonning RG4 6UT
T: 0118 9692277 **F:** 0118 9441296
E: greathouse@btconnect.com
www.greathouseatsonning.co.uk
40 £119 8 £119 (£119)
4 £149 7 £60 V
Mastercard, Visa, American Express,
Delta, Diners Club International ★★★
All rooms en-suite

CHARVIL

SU7775 1.3miles (2km)
Twyford 1.6miles (2.6km)PF

S M T W T F S   S M T W T F S

S M T W T F S   S M T W T F S

Pubs: Lands End 0118 934 0700 & Wee
Waif 0118 9440066

Wee Waif Lodge

Mr Kevin Bungay
Old Bath Road, Charvil RG10 9JR
T: 0118 9440066 **F:** 0118 9691525
www.weewaif.tablesir.com
32 £65 10 £65 (£65)
28 £80 V
Mastercard, Visa, American Express,
Delta ★★All rooms en-suite and some
non-smoking.

WARGRAVE

SU7878 3.1miles (5km)
Wargrave

S M T W T F S   S M T W T F S

S M T W T F S

Appletree Cottage

Mrs Trish Langham
Backsideans, Wargrave RG10 8JS
T: 0118 9404306 **M:** 07850 381076
www.appletreecottage.co.uk
1 £50 (£45) 1 £40 (min
age 10) V DRY ◆◆◆◆
All rooms en-suite
VisitBritain Silver Award.

Ischia   *Closed Xmas*

Mrs Kate Turner
Dark Lane, Wargrave RG10 8JU
T: 0118 9402886 **M:** 07778 615975
E: kasiapj@aol.com
1 £55 (£40) 2 £65 (min
age 10) V DRY All rooms
en-suite

LOWER SHIPLAKE

 **SU7779** 🏠 on path
🍺 **Shiplake PF** 📞

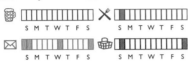

Pub: Baskerville Arms 0118 9403332. For further information visit www. shiplake.net

---

INN | **The Baskerville**   *Closed Xmas Day*

Mr Cromack
Station Road, Lower Shiplake RG9 3NY
T: 0118 9403332
E: enquiries@thebaskerville.com
www.thebaskerville.com
🛏 3 £75 🛏 1 £75 (£65) 🛏 1 £85 🛏 1 £45 ⊘ ⭐ 📺 V 🔥 🅾 💳
Mastercard, Visa, Delta ◆◆◆◆
All rooms en-suite.

HENLEY-ON-THAMES

 **SU7682** 🏠 on path
🚂 **Henley-on-Thames**

Town with full range of services, visit www.visit-henley.org.uk for further details. Henley has a wide range of accommodation – details from Tourist Information Centre (see section introduction).

☆ River and Rowing Museum
T: 01491 415600 **E:** museum@rrm.co.uk
www.rrm.co.uk

Lenwade

3 Western Road,
Henley-on-Thames RG9 1JL

A delightful Victorian home offering 5 star accommodation in a quiet residential road with parking. Ideally located 10 mins. walk from the Thames Path, shops, restaurants station etc. Superb freshly cooked breakfasts and buffet table. As members of The Walkers Charter we are astutely aware of your needs. A very warm welcome awaits.

Tel: 01491 573468/ Fax: 01491 411664
Email: lenwadeuk@aol.com
www.w3b-ink.com/lenwade

Section 9

Henley-on-Thames to Marlow

The pleasures of this 9 miles (14km) stretch of the Path lie in walking beside the now mature river surrounded by the wooded slopes of the Chiltern Hills. There are likely to be more people enjoying the Path and river than on previous sections but it's rarely very busy

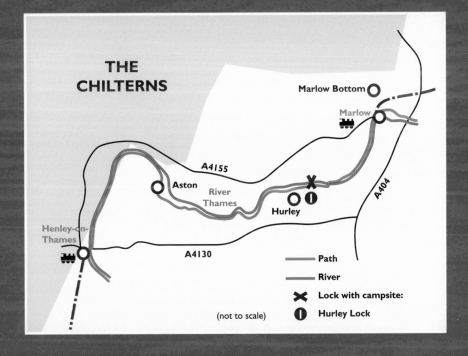

THE CHILTERNS

Marlow Bottom

Marlow

A4155

Aston

River Thames

Hurley

Henley-on-Thames

A4130

A404

Path

River

Lock with campsite:

Hurley Lock

(not to scale)

Maps

Landranger maps	175	Reading & Windsor
Explorer maps	171	Chiltern Hills West
	172	Chiltern Hills East

Taxi Services

Place	Name	Telephone numbers
Henley	Chiltern Taxis	01491 578899
Henley	County Cars	01491 579696
Henley	Harris Taxis	01491 577036
Henley	Talbot Taxis	01491 574000
Marlow	Cresta Cars	01628 476395
Marlow	Marlow Express Cars	01628 487722

Car Parks

The following is a list of public car parks close to the Thames Path and does not include on-street parking in villages or towns. Where there are several car parks in a town, those closest to the Path have been listed. Unfortunately theft from vehicles parked in the countryside does occasionally occur, so please leave valuables you don't want to carry at home.

Place	Map Grid Reference
Henley-on-Thames, Mill Lane	SU 771817
Henley-on-Thames, Mill Meadows	SU 766822
Mill End, south of Hambleden off A4122 (cross the river via Hambleden weir)	SU 785855
Hurley	SU 825841
Marlow, Pound Lane	SU 849863
Marlow, Gossmore recreation grounds	SU 858861

Toilets

Place	Map Grid Reference
Henley-on-Thames, Mill Meadows ♿	SU 766822
Mill End car park ♿, south of Hambleden (cross the river via Hambleden weir)	SU 785855
Hurley Lock	SU 826843
Temple Lock	SU 837844
Marlow, Higginson Park ♿	SU 850863
Marlow Lock	SU 855860

Tourist Information Centres

* Offers accommodation booking service for personal callers during opening hours.

Place

Address/Opening Hours

*Henley-on-Thames

King's Arms Barn, Kings Road, Henley-on-Thames RG9 2DG
T: 01491 578034 **F**: 01491 411766
E: henleyvic@frenchjones.co.uk
www.visithenley-on-thames.co.uk

Opening hours:
Summer: (Mar 31-Sep 30) daily 10:00-17:00
Winter: (Oct 1-Mar 31) daily 10:00-16:00

*Marlow

31 High Street, Marlow SL7 1AU
T: 01628 483597 **F**: 01628 471915
E: tourism_enquiries@wycombe.gov.uk

Opening hours:
Summer: (Easter-Sep 30) Mon-Fri 9:00-17:00; Sat 9:30-17:00;
Winter: (Oct 1-Easter) Mon-Fri 9:00-17:00; Sat 9:30-16:00

ASTON

SU7884 on path

Henley-on-Thames 2.8miles (4.5km)

S M T W T F S   S M T W T F S

Pub: Flower Pot Hotel 01491 574721

HURLEY

SU8285 on path

Marlow 3.7miles (6km)

WC

S M T W T F S   S M T W T F S

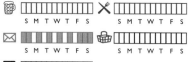
S M T W T F S   S M T W T F S

S M T W T F S

Meadow View

Ms Linda Proctor
Henley Road, Hurley SL6 5LW
T/F: 01628 829764 **M:** 07702 275612
E: linproctor@meadowviewhurley.
fsworld.co.uk
2 £60 ✖✖ (min age 10) **V**
★★★★★ Some rooms
en-suite
VisitBritain Silver Award. Packed
lunches/evening meals by prior
arrangement only

Hurley Bed & Breakfast
Closed Xmas & New Year

Mrs Katie Gear
The Old Farm House, High Street,
Hurley SL6 5NB
T: 01628 825446
E: info@hurleybedandbreakfast.co.uk
www.hurleybedandbreakfast.co.uk
3 £60 2 £60 (£55) 3 £55
V DRY Mastercard, Visa, Delta
◆◆◆◆ All rooms en-suite

Hurley Riverside Park   *Closed Nov-March*

Mrs Louise Bond
Park Office, Hurley SL6 5NE
T: 01628 823501   **F:** 01628 825533
E: info@hurleyriversidepark.co.uk
www.hurleyriversidepark.co.uk
62 £8 124 £9
WC CG
Mastercard, Visa, Delta ★★★★
Self-catering accommodation
available from £180 per week

Hurley Lock   *Closed Oct-March*

The Lockkeeper
Mill Lane, Hurley SL6 1SA
T: 01628 824334
10

MARLOW

SU8586 👢 on path
🚃 Marlow

Town with full range of services; visit www.marlowtown.co.uk for further details. Marlow has a wide range of accommodation – details from Tourist Information Centre (see section introduction).

8 Firview Close

2 rooms, double and twin
£55 (£40).
Friendly informal house
5 mins from the river.

*Tel: Mrs Pauline King
01628 485735*

*8 Firview Close
Marlow SL7 1SZ*

MARLOW BOTTOM

SU8488 👢 1.9miles (3km)
🚃 Marlow 2.2miles (3.5km) 📞

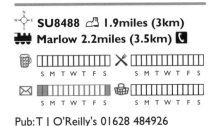

Pub: T J O'Reilly's 01628 484926

Sue Simmons Bed & Breakfast

Mrs Sue Simmons
61 Hill Farm Road, Marlow Bottom SL7 3LX
T/F: 01628 475145 **M:** 07867 547763 **E:** suesimmons@accommodationmarlow.com
www.accommodationmarlow.com
1 £65 (£40) 1 £35 🚭 ✝ V
DRY 🚗 👫 ◆◆◆

Marlow

Section 10

Marlow to Windsor

This 14 miles (22km) section travels through particularly attractive wooded countryside as far as Maidenhead. Beyond Maidenhead the river becomes busier and in places there are views of grand homes finishing with the grandest of them all, Windsor Castle, towering above the water.

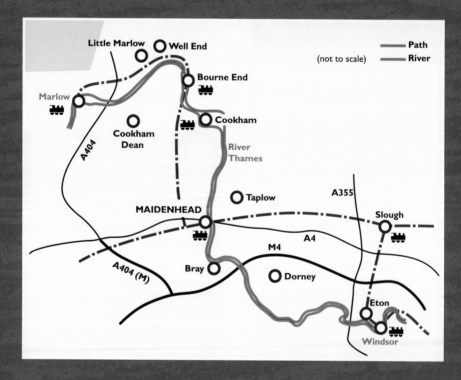

Maps

Landranger maps	175	Reading & Windsor
Explorer maps	172	Chiltern Hills East
	160	Windsor, Weybridge & Bracknell

Taxi Services

Place	Name	Telephone numbers
Marlow	Cresta Cars	01628 476395
Marlow	Marlow Express Cars	01628 487722
Bourne End	Bourne End Cars	01628 523232
Bourne End	Carlton Private Hire	01628 533111
Maidenhead	A-Z Cars	01628 621234
Maidenhead	Best Way Taxis	01628 777585
Maidenhead	Embassy Cars	01628 780052
Maidenhead	Maidenhead Taxi Rank	01628 634311
Maidenhead	Station Taxis	01628 771000
Windsor	Beaumont Taxis	01753 775075
Windsor	Five Star Car Hire	01753 859555 or 858888
Windsor	Windsor Radio Cars	01753 677677

Car Parks

The following is a list of public car parks close to the Thames Path and does not include on-street parking in villages or towns. Where there are several car parks in a town, those closest to the Path have been listed. Unfortunately theft from vehicles parked in the countryside does occasionally occur, so please leave valuables you don't want to carry at home.

Place	Map Grid Reference
Marlow, Pound Lane	SU 849863
Marlow, Gossmore recreation grounds	SU 858861
Spade Oak, west of Bourne End	SU 884876
Bourne End, Wakeman Road	SU 895874
Cookham, Sutton Road	SU 897853
Maidenhead, Hines Meadow, Crown Lane	SU 891813
Eton, Meadow Lane	SU 965773
Windsor, River Street	SU 967771

Toilets

Place	Map Grid Reference
Marlow, Higginson Park ♿	SU 850863
Marlow Lock	SU 855860
Bourne End, Wakeman Road car park ♿	SU 895874
Cookham, Sutton Road car park ♿	SU 897853
Maidenhead, various inc Mallards Reach, Bridge Avenue	SU 892812
Bray Lock	SU 798910
Boveney Lock	SU 778945
Eton Court Car Park ♿	SU 967774
Windsor, various inc Windsor & Eton Riverside Station ♿	SU 968773

Tourist Information Centres

* Offers accommodation booking service for personal callers during opening hours.

Place	Address/Opening Hours
*Marlow	31 High Street, Marlow SL7 1AU **T**: 01628 483597 **F**: 01628 471915 **E**: tourism_enquiries@wycombe.gov.uk **Opening hours:** Summer: (Easter-Sep 30) Mon-Fri 9:00-17:00; Sat 9:30-17:00 Winter: (Oct 1-Easter) Mon-Fri 9:00-17:00; Sat 9:30-16:00
*Maidenhead	The Library, St Ives Road, Maidenhead SL6 1QU **T**: 01628 796502 **F**: 01628 796971 **E**: Maidenhead.tic@rbwm.gov.uk www.maidenhead.gov.uk **Opening hours:** All year: Mon/Wed 09:30-17:00; Tues/Thurs 09:30-20:00; Fri 09:30-19:00; Sat 09:30-16:00
*Windsor	Old Booking Hall, 24 High Street, Windsor SL4 1LH **T**: 01753 743900 (general information) 01753 743907 (accommodation bookings) **F**: 01753 743904 www.windsor.gov.uk **Opening hours:** All year: Mon-Sun 10:00-17:00 (subject to seasonal changes)

COOKHAM DEAN

SU8785 🥾 2 miles (3.2km)
🚃 Cookham Rise 1.4miles
(2.2km) 📞

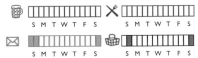

For further information visit
www.cookham.com

Cartlands Cottage

Mr & Mrs R Parkes
Kings Lane, Cookham Dean SL6 9AY
T: 01628 482196

🛏 1 £50 (£35) 🚭 ✦✦ V 🔥 **DRY** 🔥
◆◆ Room is en-suite
🔥 Room can be also single/family
as required, price on application.
Accommodation is Marlow side of
village.

🏠 The Inn on the Green

Mrs Deslandes
The Old Cricket Common, Cookham
Dean SL6 9NZ
T: 01628 482638 **F:** 01628 487474
M: 07779 990830
E: reception@theinnonthegreen.com
www.theinnonthegreen.com

🛏 9 £90 ✦✦ ♿ 🔥 V 🅾 VISA
Mastercard, Visa, American Express,
Delta. All rooms en-suite.

LITTLE MARLOW

SU8787 🥾 0.6miles (1km)
🚃 Bourne End 1.7miles (2.7km)
PF 📞

☆ Enid Blyton's House, The Old Thatch
T: 01628 527518

Old Barn Cottage

Mrs Anthea Falk
Church Road, Little Marlow SL7 3RZ
T: 01628 483817
E: anthea@oldbarncottage.co.uk
www.oldbarncottage.co.uk

🛏 1 £45 (£35) 🚭 ✦✦ 🔥 V 🔥 **DRY**
🔥 �car ◆◆◆◆ Room is en-suite

WELL END

SU8887 🥾 0.2miles (0.4km)
🚃 Bourne End 0.8miles (1.2km) 📞

Pub: Spade Oak 01628 520090

☆ Spade Oak Lake Nature Reserve

BOURNE END

 SU8987 on path
Bourne End

Small town with range of services

COOKHAM

SU8985 on path
Cookam Rise 1mile (1.6km) [phone]
[icon] [wc]WC

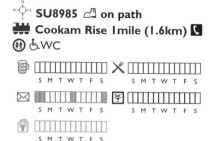

For further information visit
www.cookham.com

☆ Stanley Spencer Gallery
T: 01628 471885
www.stanleyspencer.org.uk

MAIDENHEAD

SU8981 on path
Maidenhead Central

Town with full range of services; visit
www.maidenhead.net for further
details. Maidenhead has a wide range
of accommodation – details from
Tourist Information Centre (see section
introduction).

TAPLOW

 SU9082 1.1mile (1.8km)
Taplow 0.8miles (1.2km) [phone]

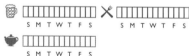

☆ Cliveden - National Trust property
overlooking the Thames
T: 01494 755562 **F:** 01628 669461
E: cliveden@ntrust.org.uk
www.nationaltrust.org.uk

Cliveden House [H]

The Manager
Taplow SL6 0JF
T: 01628 668561 **F:** 01628 661837
E: info@clivedenhouse.co.uk
www.clivedenhouse.co.uk
[icon] 4 £300 [icon] 6 £400 [icon] 3 £230
[icons]
[VISA] Mastercard, Visa, American Express,
Delta ◆◆◆◆ All rooms en-suite
[!] Prices not inclusive of VAT

Amerden Caravan & Camping Park   *Closed Jan-March*   [A] SC

Mrs Hakesley
Old Marsh Lane, Taplow SL6 0EE
T: 01628 627461
E: beverly@amerdencaravanpark.co.uk
[A] 30 £6 [caravan] 30 £14 [icons]
[wc]WC [icons] CG ★★★★
[!] Self-catering accommodation
available from £250/week

Bridge Cottage Guest House
Closed Xmas & New Year

Mr & Mrs M Staszewski
Bath Road, Taplow SL6 0AR
T: 01628 626805 **F:** 01628 788785
E: bridgecottagebb@aol.com
www.bridgecottagebb.co.uk

 3 £57 2 £62 (£52) 1 £78
1 £38 ✿✦ ♿ V DRY ◆◆◆

Some rooms en-suite

BRAY

 **SU9079** 1.3miles (2km)
Maidenhead Central 1.6miles
(2.5km) PF ♿WC

🍺 ⫿⫿⫿⫿⫿⫿⫿⫿⫿⫿⫿ ✗ ⫿⫿⫿⫿⫿⫿⫿⫿⫿⫿⫿⫿⫿
   S M T W T F S   S M T W T F S
⫿⫿⫿⫿⫿⫿⫿⫿⫿⫿⫿⫿
   S M T W T F S

The Old Coach House

Mrs Fiona Stewart
3 Windsor Road, Braywick SL6 1UZ
T: 01628 671244 **F:** 01628 625272
www.oldcoachhouse.biz

2 £60 (£40) 2 £40 ✿✦ (min
age 3) V DRY Some rooms en-suite

DORNEY & DORNEY REACH

SU9379 0.9miles (1.5km)
Taplow 1.7miles (2.7km)PF

🍺 ⫿⫿⫿⫿⫿⫿⫿⫿⫿⫿⫿⫿ ✗ ⫿⫿⫿⫿⫿⫿⫿⫿⫿⫿⫿⫿
   S M T W T F S   S M T W T F S
🫖 ⫿⫿⫿⫿⫿⫿⫿⫿⫿⫿⫿⫿
   S M T W T F S

Pubs: Palmers Arms 01628 666612 &
Pineapple 01628 662353

☆ Dorney Court
T: 01628 604638 **F:** 01628 665772
E: palmer@dorneycourt.co.uk
www.dorneycourt.co.uk

☆ Jubilee River with various
recreational opportunities
www.environment-agency.gov.uk

ETON

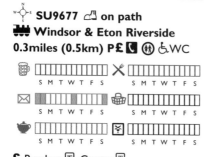

SU9677 🥾 on path
Windsor & Eton Riverside
0.3miles (0.5km) P£ 📞 ⚥ ♿WC

	S M T W T F S	✖	S M T W T F S
	S M T W T F S		S M T W T F S
✉	S M T W T F S	⛟	S M T W T F S
☕	S M T W T F S	⚔	S M T W T F S

£ Barclays 🏧, Coutts 🏧

INN **Crown and Cushion Inn**
Closed Xmas Eve & Day

Mr Robert Tindall
84 High Street, Eton SL4 6AF
T: 01753 861531 **M:** 07968 538714
E: rwt2243@msn.com
🛏 8 £59 (59) 🚭 VISA Mastercard, Visa,
Delta ★★★★Some rooms en-suite.

WINDSOR

SU9676 🥾 on path
Windsor Central

Town with full range of services;
visit www.windsor.gov.uk for further
details. Windsor has a wide range of
accommodation – details from Tourist
Information Centre (see section
introduction).

☆ Windsor Castle
T: 020 7766 7304 www.royal.gov.uk

☆ LEGOLAND® Windsor
T: 08705 040404 **F:** 01753 626200
E: sales@legoland.co.uk
www.legoland.co.uk

☆ Savill Garden
T: 01753 847518 **F:** 01753 847536
E: savillgarden@crownestate.org.uk
www.savillgarden.co.uk

Windsor

Section
11

Windsor to Shepperton

As the Thames Path gets closer to London the number of
riverside settlements inevitably increase, but along this 14
miles (22km) section there are still considerable amounts of
green space to enjoy before reaching Shepperton.

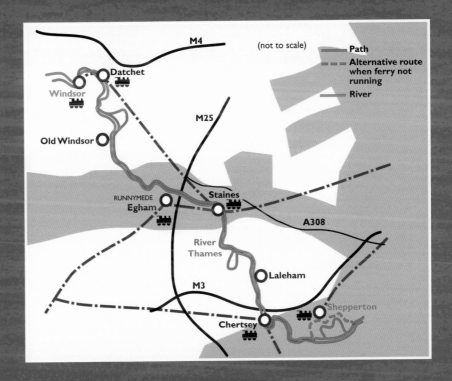

M4

(not to scale)

— Path
— — Alternative route
when ferry not
running
— River

Datchet

Windsor

M25

Old Windsor

RUNNYMEDE
Egham

Staines

A308

River
Thames

M3

Laleham

Chertsey

Shepperton

Maps

Landranger maps	175	Reading & Windsor
	176	West London
Explorer maps	160	Windsor, Weybridge & Bracknell

Taxi Services

Place	Name	Telephone numbers
Windsor	Beaumont Taxis	01753 775075
Windsor	Five Star Car Hire	01753 859555 or 858888
Windsor	Windsor Radio Cars	01753 677677
Egham	Egham Taxis	01784 433933
Egham	A Line Taxis	01784 430609
Egham	Arrow Cars	01784 436533
Egham	Gemini Cars	01784 432468
Chertsey	Abbey Cars	01932 568055

Car Parks

The following is a list of public car parks close to the Thames Path and does not include on-street parking in villages or towns. Where there are several car parks in a town, those closest to the Path have been listed. Unfortunately theft from vehicles parked in the countryside does occasionally occur, so please leave valuables you don't want to carry at home.

Place	Map Grid Reference
Windsor, River Street	SU 967771
Romney Lock	SU 970776
Windsor Home Park	SU 972778
Runnymede National Trust (April to end September)	SU 995733
Runnymede Pleasure Grounds	TQ 007724
Staines, Bridge Street	TQ 032716
Laleham	TQ 051686
Laleham Park, Thameside	TQ 053677
Chertsey Bridge	TQ 055666
Shepperton Lock	TQ 072660

Toilets

Place	Map Grid Reference
Windsor, various inc Windsor & Eton Riverside Station ♿	SU 968773
Romney Lock	SU 970776
Runnymede Pleasure Grounds ♿	TQ 007724
Bell Weir Lock	TQ 017721
Staines, various inc Thames Street ♿	TQ 036714
Laleham Park, Thameside ♿	TQ 053677
Shepperton Lock ♿	TQ 072660

Tourist Information Centres

* Offers accommodation booking service for personal callers during opening hours.

Place

Address/Opening Hours

*Windsor

Old Booking Hall, 24 High Street, Windsor SL4 1LH
T: 01753 743900 (general information)
01753 743907 (accommodation bookings) **F**: 01753 743904
www.windsor.gov.uk

Opening hours:
All year: Mon-Sun 10:00-17:00 (subject to seasonal changes)

Runnymede Memorial

DATCHET

SU9876 on path
Datchet PF ☎

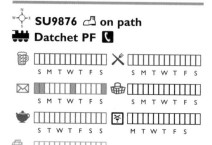

£ Nationwide ✉

OLD WINDSOR

SU9874 on path
Datchet 1.9miles (3km) PF ☎

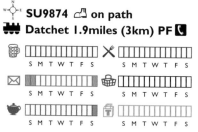

£ HSBC ✉

Visit www.windsor.gov.uk for further details

INN | The Union Inn

Mr F W Ward
Crimp Hill, Old Windsor SL4 2QY
T: 01753 861955 **F:** 01753 831378
www.unioninnwindsor.co.uk
🛏 8 £70 4 £55 👫 ♿ V ◑ 💳
Mastercard, Visa, American Express,
Delta ★★★★ All rooms en-suite.
ℍ Prices are reduced on Friday and
Saturday nights.

EGHAM

TO0171 on path
Egham 0.7miles (1.2km)

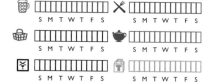

T: 01753 743 900 **F:** 01753 743 904
E: windsor.tic@bwn.gov.uk
www.windsor.gov.uk

Wildings Beauvilla   *Closed Xmas*

Mrs Jo Wilding
44 Grange Road, Egham TW20 9QP
T: 01784 435115 **M:** 07793 555255
E: jowilding@ntlworld.com
🛏 2 £50 2 £50 (£40) 1 £30
🚭 👫 ♿ 🖼 V Some rooms en-suite

STAINES

TO0371 on path
Staines

Town with wide range of services and
accommodation: visit
www.stainesweb.co.uk for further
information

LALEHAM

TQ0568  **on path**
🚂 Staines 2.1miles (3.4km) PF 📞

🍺 |||||||||| ✕ ||||||||||
    S M T W T F S   S M T W T F S

⚑ Laleham Camping Club
Closed Oct-Mar

The Warden
Laleham Park, Thameside TW18 1SS
T: 01932 564149   **F:** 01932 569992
⚑ 125 £5 🚐 125 £5 🔌 🚿 🚽 ♿
&WC 🖥 🖲

❚ Prices per person. For caravans, add
£1.50 hook up fee.

CHERTSEY

TQ0466 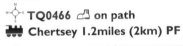 **on path**
🚂 Chertsey 1.2miles (2km) PF

🍺 ||||||||||||| ✕ |||||||||||
   S M T W T F S   S M T W T F S

✉ |||||||||||| 🍱 |||||||||||
   S M T W T F S   S M T W T F S

Visit www.chertsey.org.uk for further
details

Chertsey Camping & Caravanning Club ⚑

The Site Manager
Bridge Road, Chertsey KT16 8JX
T: 01932 562405
www.campingandcaravanningclub.co.uk
⚑ 100 £18 🚐 100 £18 🔌 🚿 🚽 ♿
&WC 🖥 📞 🖲 CG 💳 Mastercard,
Visa, Delta ★★★★
❚ Prices for two people

SHEPPERTON

TO0867  **on path**
🚂 Shepperton

Town with a full range of services, but
the accommodation below particularly
welcomes Thames Path walkers.

Forty Winks

Mr M Potts
47 Burbidge Road, Shepperton TW17
0ED
T: 01932 224963 **M:** 07814 048640
🛏 1 £50 (£40) 🛏 1 £50 🛏 1 £30
👪 🔌 🖲 🚗 🚶

Splash Cottage

Mr Malcolm Shaw
91 Watersplash Road, Shepperton
TW17 0EE
T: 01932 229987
E: info@lazy-river.co.uk
www.lazy-river.co.uk
🛏 1 £50 🛏 1 £50 (£30) 🛏 1 £30
🚭 👪 (min age 9) V 🧺 DRY

Section 12

Shepperton to Teddington

This section is remarkably varied and includes vast reservoirs, an old racecourse, a royal palace and smart Kingston. It is the last non-tidal stretch of the Path as beyond Teddington Lock the River Thames is tidal.

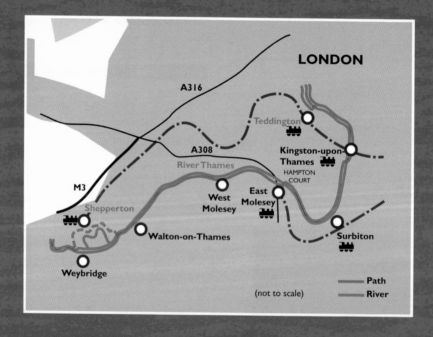

Maps

Landranger maps	176	West London
Explorer maps	160	Windsor, Weybridge & Bracknell
	161	London South

Taxi Services

Place	Name	Telephone numbers
Weybridge	AGM Cars	01932 858585
Weybridge	Apple Cars Ltd	01932 568686
Weybridge	Eden Cars	01932 830830
Walton-on-Thames	Walton Station Taxis	01932 230830
Walton-on-Thames	Swan Cars	01932 230830
East Molesey	Headway Cars	01784 471111
East Molesey	The Pack of Cars	020 8941 7070

Car Parks

The following is a list of public car parks close to the Thames Path and does not include on-street parking in villages or towns. Where there are several car parks in a town, those closest to the Path have been listed. Unfortunately theft from vehicles parked in the countryside does occasionally occur, so please leave valuables you don't want to carry at home.

Place	Map Grid Reference
Shepperton Lock	TQ 072660
Walton Bridge	TQ 094664
Molesey, Hurst Park	TQ 143693
Hampton Wick, by Kingston Bridge	TQ 176695
Kingston-upon-Thames, various	

Toilets

Place	Map Grid Reference
Shepperton Lock &	TQ 072660
Walton Bridge &	TQ 094664
Molesey Lock &	TQ 153686
Kingston-upon-Thames, various	

Tourist Information Centres

* Offers accommodation booking service for personal callers during opening hours.

Place

Address/Opening Hours

Kingston-upon-Thames

Market House, Market Place,
Kingston upon Thames KT1 1JS
T: 0181 547 5592 **F**: 0181 547 5594
E: tourist.information@rbk.kingston.gov.uk
www.kingston.gov.uk.

Opening hours:
All year: Mon-Fri 10:00-17:00; Sat 9:00-16:00

*Richmond

Old Town Hall, Whittaker Avenue, Richmond TW9 1TP
T: 0181 940 9125 **F**: 0181 940 6899
www.visitrichmond.co.uk

Opening hours:
Summer: (May 1-Oct 31) Mon-Sat 10:00-17:00;
Sun 10:30-13:30
Winter: (Nov 1-Apr 30) Mon-Sat 10:00-17:00

WEYBRIDGE

TQ0764 on path
Weybridge 1.2miles (2km)

Town with a full range of services, but
the accommodation below particularly
welcomes Thames Path walkers.

Riverdene Gardens
Closed Xmas, New Year & Easter

Mrs Emilia Nunn
1oatlands Drive, Weybridge KT13 9NA
T/F: 01932 223574 **M:** 07979 817340
E: riverdenegardens@btinternet.com
www.riverdenegardens.co.uk
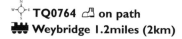 4 £75 1 £90 (£90) 1 £90
(min age 3) **V** Mastercard,
Visa, ◆◆◆◆◆ All rooms en-suite.
VisitBritain Silver Award

WALTON-ON-THAMES

TO1066 on path
Walton-on-Thames

Town with a full range of services, but
the accommodation below particularly
welcomes Thames Path walkers.

The Cottage

Mrs Pat Sims
52 Bridge Street, Walton-on-Thames
KS12 1AP
T: 01932 242576
E: thecottage@tvpsurrey.co.uk
 1 £60 1 £60 (£40) 1 £35
V DRY Some rooms en-suite.

MOLESEY

TQ1368 on path
Hampton Court

Town with a full range of services, but the accommodation below particularly welcomes Thames Path walkers.

SC **Wisteria Cottage**

Ms Jenny Bailey
11 Riverside Avenue, East Molesey
KT8 0AE
T: 0208 3391278
E: jenny@riversiderentals.co.uk
www.riversiderentals.co.uk
DRY Mastercard, Visa, Delta, Switch ★★★★
Prices from £200 per week

SURBITON

TQ1867 1.3miles (2km)

Town with a full range of services, but the accommodation below particularly welcomes Thames Path walkers.

Ditton Lodge Hotel

Mrs R Malakouti
47 Lovelace Road, Long Ditton KT6 6NA
T: 0208 3997482 **F:** 0208 2241897 **E:** info@dittonlodge.co.uk
www.dittonlodge.co.uk
10 £72 (£64) 4 £54 V
Mastercard, Visa, Delta ◆◆◆◆
All rooms en-suite.
Rooms can be twin/double/family as required.

21 Cotterill Road

Mrs Jennifer Booth
21 Cotterill Road, Surbiton KT6 7UW
T: 0208 3990955 **M:** 07971 670486
E: jenniferbooth@hotmail.co.uk
1 £50 2 £30 V DRY

KINGSTON-UPON-THAMES

TQ1869 on path
Kingston-upon-Thames

Outer London - full range of services available. Kingston has a wide range of accommodation – details from Tourist Information Centre (see section introduction).

TEDDINGTON

TQ1671 on path
Teddington

Outer London - full range of services available. Contact Kingston Tourist Information Centre for further information (see section introduction)

Section 13

LONDON: Teddington to Putney

From Teddington the Thames Path offers a choice of walking routes either side of the river as far as Island Gardens on the Isle of Dogs. The south bank along this section (12 miles/19km) has a surprisingly rural feel, and the north bank (14 miles/23km) too has several lengthy green stretches. Whichever route is taken, there's an enormous amount to see and visit.

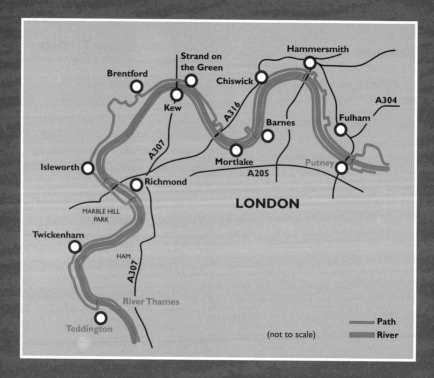

Maps

Landranger maps	176	West London
Explorer maps	161	London South

Car Parks

Between Teddington and Putney there are a number of parking opportunities. Walkers are advised not to use their cars if at all possible - public transport is widely available and there is also a congestion charge which is now in force for those who drive into central London.

Tourist Information Centres

* Offers accommodation booking service for personal callers during opening hours.

Place
Address/Opening Hours

*Richmond
Old Town Hall, Whittaker Avenue, Richmond TW9 1TP
T: 0181 940 9125 **F**: 0181 940 6899
www.visitrichmond.co.uk

Opening hours:
Summer: (May 1-Oct 31) Mon-Sat 10:00-17:00;
Sun 10:30-13:30
Winter: (Nov 1-Apr 30) Mon-Sat 10:00-17:00

TEDDINGTON TO PUTNEY

Full range of services and accommodation available. Visit www.visitlondon.com for further information

Richmond

Section

14

LONDON: Putney to Tower Bridge

This is a relatively short section (11 miles/17km along the
south bank and 10 miles/16km on the north bank) but one
packed with the fascinating history of London. Virtually the
whole of the route is built up but there is a range of old and
modern architecture to enjoy and the odd patch of green to sit
in and to enjoy the river.

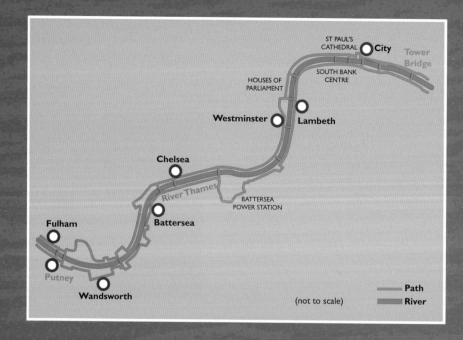

ST PAUL'S
CATHEDRAL City

Tower
Bridge

SOUTH BANK
CENTRE

HOUSES OF
PARLIAMENT

Westminster Lambeth

Chelsea

River Thames

BATTERSEA
POWER STATION

Fulham

Battersea

Putney

Wandsworth

(not to scale)

Path

River

Maps

Landranger maps	176	West London
Explorer maps	161	London South
	173	London North

Car Parks

Between Putney and Tower Bridge there are a number of parking opportunities. Walkers are advised not to use their cars if at all possible - public transport is widely available and there is also a congestion charge which is now in force for those who drive into central London.

Tourist Information Centres

* Offers accommodation booking service for personal callers during opening hours.

Place
*Britain and London Visitor Centre

Address/Opening Hours
1 Lower Regent Street, London SW1 4XT
T: 08701 566 366
www.visitbritain.com

Opening hours:
Mon 9.30am-6.30pm; Tues-Fri 9am-6.30pm;
Sat (October-May) 10am-4pm; Sat (June-Sept) 9am-5pm;
Sun 10am-4pm

*Southwark

Level 2 Information Desk, Tate Modern, Bankside SE1 9TG
T: 020 7401 5266
E: tourisminfo@southwark.gov.uk
www.visitsouthwark.com

Opening hours:
All year: 10:00-18:00 daily

PUTNEY TO TOWER BRIDGE

Full range of services and accommodation available. Visit www.visitlondon.com for further information

 ### Earl's Court YHA

The Manager
38 Bolton Gardens, Earl's Court SW5 0AQ
T: 0870 7705804 **F:** 0870 7705805
E: earlscourt@yha.org.uk
www.yha.org.uk
🚭 ✝(min age 3) ⏣ 💳 Visa, Mastercard, Delta, Switch, Solo, Maestro
★★★
Rooms from double to 10 beds. Prices from £19.50 per adult

 ### Holland House YHA

The Manager
Holland Walk, Kensington W8 7QU
T: 0870 7705866 **F:** 0870 7705867
E: hollandhouse@yha.org.uk
www.yha.org.uk
✝(min age 3) V 🖐️🕭 ⏣ 💳 Visa, Mastercard, Delta, Switch, Solo, Maestro
★★★
Rooms from 6 to 20 beds. Prices from £21.60 per adult

 ### Oxford Street YHA

The Manager
14 Noel Street W1F 3PD
T: 0870 7705984 **F:** 0207 7341657
E: oxfordst@yha.org.uk
www.yha.org.uk
🚭 ✝(min age 3) V ⏣ 💳 Visa, Mastercard, Delta, Switch, Solo, Maestro
★★
Rooms from double to 4 beds. Prices from £23.50 per adult

St Pancras YHA

The Manager
79-81 Euston Road NW1 2QE
T: 0870 7706044 **F:** 0207 3886766
E: stpancras@yha.org.uk
www.yha.org.uk
🚭 ✝🕭V 🖐️🕭 ⏣ 💳 Visa, Mastercard, Delta, Switch, Solo, Maestro
★★★★ Some rooms en-suite.
Rooms from double to 6 beds. Prices from £24.60 per adult

St Pauls YHA

The Manager
36 Carter Lane EC4V 5AB
T: 0870 7705764 **F:** 0207 2367681
E: stpauls@yha.org.uk
www.yha.org.uk
🚭 ✝V 🖐️🕭 ⏣ 💳 Visa, Mastercard, Delta, Switch, Solo, Maestro ★★★
Rooms from single to 15 beds. Prices from £25.50 per adult

Section 15

LONDON: Tower Bridge to Thames Barrier

The Thames Path offers a choice of walking routes either side of the river along this section as far as Island Gardens on the Isle of Dogs opposite Greenwich (10 miles/16km on the south bank and 5miles/9km along the north bank). This is a section of old and new with some hidden corners still to find where it's possible to imagine what it was like when London was the busiest port in the world.

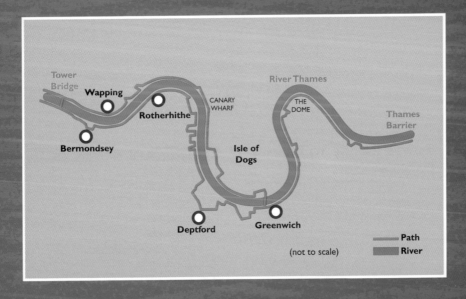

Tower Bridge

Wapping

Rotherhithe

CANARY WHARF

River Thames

THE DOME

Thames Barrier

Bermondsey

Isle of Dogs

Deptford

Greenwich

(not to scale)

━━━ **Path**

▬▬▬ **River**

Maps

Landranger maps	177	East London
Explorer maps	173	London North
	162	Greenwich & Gravesend

Car Parks

Between Tower Bridge and the Thames Barrier there are a number of parking opportunities. Walkers are advised not to use their cars if at all possible - public transport is widely available and there is also a congestion charge which is now in force for those who drive into central London.

Tourist Information Centres

* Offers accommodation booking service for personal callers during opening hours.

Place   **Address/Opening Hours**

*Southwark

Level 2 Information Desk, Tate Modern, Bankside SE1 9TG
T: 020 7401 5266
E: tourisminfo@southwark.gov.uk
www.visitsouthwark.com

Opening hours:
All year: 10:00-18:00 daily

*Greenwich

Pepys House, 2 Cutty Sark Gardens, Greenwich,
London SE10 9LW. **T**: 0870 608 2000 **F**: 0208 853 4607

E: tic@greenwich.gov.uk
www.greenwich.gov.uk

Opening hours:
All year: Daily 10:00-17:00

TOWER BRIDGE TO THAMES BARRIER

Full range of services and accommodation available. Visit www.visitlondon.com for further information

Thameside YHA

The Manager
20 Salter Rd, Rotherhithe SE16 5PR
T: 0870 7706010 **F**: 0207 2372919
E: thameside@yha.org.uk
www.yha.org.uk
🚭 ♿✜♿.V 🛁♥🔟 💳 Visa,
Mastercard, Delta, Switch, Solo, Maestro
★★ All rooms en-suite.
◨ Rooms from double to 10 beds.
Prices from £20 per adult

INDEX OF PLACES

Distances between places along the Thames Path in kilometres

London North Bank

Teddington	Putney	Tower Bridge	Greenwich
22.7	Putney		
37.6	14.9	Tower Bridge	
45.8	23.1	8.2	Greenwich

London South Bank

Teddington	Putney	Tower Bridge	Greenwich	Thames Barrier
18.3	Putney			
33.9	15.6	Tower Bridge		
43.3	25.0	9.4	Greenwich	
50.3	32.0	16.4	7.0	Thames Barrier

Source	Cricklade	Lechlade	Newbridge	Oxford	Abingdon	Wallingford	Tilehurst	Henley	Marlow	Windsor	Shepperton	Teddington
19.8	Cricklade											
37.3	17.5	Lechlade										
63.9	44.1	26.6	Newbridge									
86.4	66.6	49.1	22.5	Oxford								
102.1	82.3	64.8	38.2	15.7	Abingdon							
123.7	103.9	86.4	59.8	37.3	21.6	Wallingford						
147.5	127.7	110.2	83.6	61.1	45.4	23.8	Tilehurst					
167.3	147.5	130.0	103.4	80.9	65.2	43.6	19.8	Henley				
181.1	161.3	143.8	117.2	94.7	79.0	57.4	33.6	13.8	Marlow			
204.1	184.3	166.8	140.2	117.7	102.0	80.4	56.6	36.8	23.0	Windsor		
226.2	206.4	188.9	162.3	139.8	124.1	102.5	78.7	58.9	45.1	21.1	Shepperton	
243.8	224.0	206.5	179.9	157.4	141.7	120.1	96.3	76.5	62.7	39.7	17.6	Teddington